Hear Me Because I Hear You:

Quickly Improve the Effectiveness of Your Relationship Communication With Simple, Time Tested Tools

TABLE OF CONTENTS

Part 1: How is the Communication in
Your Relationship? ---------------------------------- 7

Test YOUR Relationship to See
…if You NEED This Book ------------------------- 7

From Where We Started,
How Did We Get Here? ---------------------------- 9

Do YOU Need This Book for
Your Relationship? --------------------------------- 13

     1- "Communication Rot" Test:
        Do You Have It? -------------------------- 14
     2- "Stages of Kissing" Test:
        What Does Kissing Reveal? ----------- 16
     3- "Trust Metrics" Test:
        Is There Genuine Trust? ---------------- 19
     4- "Trade Off" Test:
        Happier Together than Apart? -------- 22

What You Need to Know About
Romantic Communication -------------------------- 25

    Two Basic Human Needs
        in Communication --------------------------- 25
    Three Part Romantic
        Communication Formula ------------------ 27
    About the Importance of the
        Relationship Filter -------------------------- 32

Identifying Issues Which BLOCK YOUR
Communication -- 35

    Are You Friends with Your Mate? -------------- 35
    Do You Both Understand One Another? ----- 38
    Are You Both Honest with One Another? ---- 40
    Do You Both Mate Love Each Other? -------- 41
    Are You and Your Mate Open? ----------------- 43
    Do You Both Share Decisions? ---------------- 45
    Are You Both Happy in Loving? ---------------- 47
    Common Sources of Conflict -------------------- 48

Part 2: How to Improve Communication in
Your Relationship ------------------------------------- 51

Love, Honor, and Cherish Through
Better Communication ------------------------------- 51

    How to Get the Most Out of This Book ------ 52
    Misconceptions About Romance -------------- 53
    About the Impossible Double Bind ------------ 55
    Myths of Romantic Conflict Resolution ------- 56

The Master Communication Formula ----------- 59

   Formula Part 1: AAA Technique
        to Create A+++ Relationships ---------- 59
    Ex: Resolving MONEY Conflicts ------------- 62
    Ex: Resolving PARENTING Conflicts ------- 67
    Ex: Resolving INTIMACY Conflicts ---------- 72
    Ex: Resolving WORK-LIFE Conflicts -------- 77
   Formula Part 2: About Listening ---------------- 82
   Formula Part 3: About Speaking --------------- 87
   Formula Part 4: Increasing Effectiveness ---- 90

Fighting Fair: Resolving Conflicts Peacefully -- 92

   Fighting Fair Part 1: About Complaining ----- 93
   Fighting Fair Part 2: About Criticizing --------- 96
   Fighting Fair Part 3: Resolving Conflict ------- 103
   Fighting Fair Part 4: Dealing with Difficulties- 105

Making Decisions Together ------------------------ 107

   Decisions Part 1: Reaching Consensus ------ 107
   Decisions Part 2: Creating Compromise ----- 110
   Decisions Part 3: Building Cooperation ------ 112

Giving and Receiving Forgiveness -------------- 113

   Forgiveness Part 1: Charity Begins ----------- 113
   Forgiveness Part 2: Stop Keeping Score ---- 115
   Forgiveness Part 3: Cultivating Calmness -- 117
   Forgiveness Part 4: About Confession ------- 119

Tools for Loving Communication ----------------- 122

   Being a Relationship Hero ---------------------- 122
   Tools Part 1: About Compliments -------------- 124
   Tools Part 2: About Courtesy -------------------- 132
   Tools Part 3: About Compassion --------------- 136
   Tools Part 4: Be Your Mate's Friend ----------- 141
   Tools Part 5: Building Solid Relationships -- 147
   Tools Part 6: Key Messages of Love --------- 150
   Tools Part 7: 100 Romantic Texts ------------- 159

Mystery Bonus -- 167

About the Author ------------------------------------- 169

For more information visit us online at:
http://www.soulmatelovesecrets.com
Check out our Facebook Page:
https://www.facebook.com/soulmatelovesecrets

COPYRIGHTED MATERIAL

Dedication: For My Mother

Copyright © 2018 by Ellen A. Mogensen
(Pen Name: Ellen Arlene)

This publication is designed to provide information about the subject matter covered. It is sold with the understanding that neither the publisher nor the author is engaged in rendering medical, psychological, health care, or other professional advice and/or services. If the reader desires expert assistance, the reader should seek the services of a licensed professional.

The stories shared in this book are based on real events that happened to real people. All of these individuals agreed to share their story on the condition that their real identities were hidden. That is why no names are listed in this book.

All rights reserved. No part of this book may be reproduced, scanned, or distributed in any printed or electronic form without prior written permission of the author. Brief quotes from other authors were used throughout this book.

IDENTIFICATION

1. Communication Improvement
2. Marriage Relationship
3. Marital Communication
4. Marriage Problems
5. Relationship Communication

ISBN (Identification Number):
ISBN-13: 978-1720402527
ISBN-10: 1720402523

Cover Art: by Ellen A. Mogensen

PUBLISHER'S NOTE:

There are references in this book to issues creating conflict on the topic of physical intimacy between loving marriage partners. There are NO descriptions of the act whatsoever. This is a clean and wholesome approach to improving relationship communication between loving mates.

"An error does not become a mistake until you refuse to correct it." (John F. Kennedy)

Hear Me Because I Hear You

Part 1: How is the Communication in Your Relationship?

Test YOUR Relationship to See ... if You NEED This Book

"What greater thing is there for two human souls than to feel that they are joined... to strengthen each other... to be at one with each other." (George Eliot)

Before we start ask yourself... would you like it if your communication could do all this for you in your marriage (or any other) relationship?

* **Be Heard:** *What if other people, especially your mate, could listen - really listen - you?* If you want to be heard ("hear me"), then you need to listen ("I hear you") to others. If your mate is upset, if you have the right skills (the AAA method to create A+ relationships), you can use your communication to calm them down quickly. Only when another is calm, can they hear you properly.

* **Be Understood:** *What if other people, especially your mate, could understand your point of view?* If you want to be understood ("hear me"), then you need to understand others ("I hear you"). If your mate is not "getting" you, you can use AAA communication to open them up. Only when another is open, can they understand you. Only when you are open, can you understand them.

* **Build Trust:** *What if you could build more trust between you and your mate or between you and others?* You build more trust with others by compassionate AAA communication. The more others trust you, the stronger the bond between you becomes. This is especially important in long lasting relationships.

* **Gain Cooperation:** *What if you could gain the cooperation of your mate or others in your life?* You can build more connection with others through clear, consensus driven AAA communication. The more you connect with someone else, the more they are ready to support and cooperate with you.

* **Strengthen Your Relationship:** *What if every argument you have with your mate (or anyone else) could draw you closer together instead of tearing you apart?* You can improve your communication so that conflicts can be resolved fairly for both parties. You can create A+ relationships with the AAA technique.

* **Increase Your Happiness:** *What if your communication could increase your happiness?* Happiness is the goal that underlies all goals. Once you are heard and understood properly using AAA, your mate will love you more, others will end up liking you more, trusting you more, and be willing to help you more.

* **Know More Love:** *What if your communication could help you to know more love?* Love is at the core of all happiness. When you communicate with AAA, you can bring more love, more understanding, and more compassion into any situation. This can help you turn a relationship from bad o a good one.

If this is what you want in your marriage and in your life, this book is for you.

"From Where We Started, How Did We Get Here?"

"Courage is what it takes to stand up and speak; courage is also what it takes to sit down and listen." (Winston Churchill)

It always starts the same way. The client asks, *"What you do think about my relationship with my mate?"* What this question really means is *"Do you think that my relationship is in serious trouble and/or close to ending?"*

Those with satisfying relationships never ask this question. In fact, they tend to talk about their mate favorably within the first few minutes of our conversation. Those with unsatisfying relationships ask this question fearing the answer.

When I hear this question, I say, *"Just answer a few questions for me... and you will know just how healthy your romantic relationship truly is."* Usually the client is quite excited because they are longing for more clarity about their situation.

Question #1: Where did you start?
If you are married, how did you and your mate feel about one another on your wedding day? If not, how did you and your mate feel about one another when you moved in together?

Most romantic relationships start out being happy. One of the happiest days is the wedding day. Clients will say something like this about how they started. *"We were so excited about getting married. We could not keep our hands off of each other. We could tell each other everything: we loved to talk!"*

For many couples, their wedding day was their happiest day... and it goes downhill from there. Yet, it does not have to be that way. If a couple works to grow together, then their happiness can increase from their wedding day.

Question #2: What were your last three interactions with your mate?

Outside of the usual routines, how did you and your mate get along?

Most days, couples run their lives on their routines and on their habits. If this always creates conflict, then the relationship is in trouble. Apart from that, when things "come up out of the ordinary", this is when the relationship is tested.

Example - Interaction #1: The mates have agreed to visit family members. One mate pulls out at the last minute. The other mate is not surprised because their spouse has really never gotten along with their family. The mate visits their family and makes excuses for their partner. Since this has happened often, the family is not surprised. One mate feels embarrassed by their partner's absence. The other mate resents their in-laws: neither partner is happy.

In this example, the couple is disengaging and moving away from one another.

Example - Interaction #2: The mates are at the mall. They split up: one mate takes a child to buy a pair of shoes while the other takes a child to get a hair cut. When they meet up again, one mate allowed their child to get a pair of shoes with lights that the other mate disapproved of. The other mate allowed their child to skip getting a hair-cut because the child complained too much.

In this example, the couple is disengaging and moving away from one another.

Example - Interaction #3: The mates have gone out to dinner with friends. During the conversation, one mate reveals an important detail about their partner. The other mate does not like sharing such details (even if it shows them in a good light) and so they strike back by ignoring their spouse.

In this example, the couple is disengaging and moving away from one another.

Couples are always either moving toward each other or away from one another. They are either engaging with one another or disengaging with one another.

No matter how well a couple starts their relationship, if they are constantly moving away from each other and if they are often disengaging with one another, their relationship is in trouble, no doubt about it. That is how couples who were so happy in their wedding day can become miserable years later.

Question #3: When were you happier - when you started or now?
If you could get out of your marriage/commitment - as if it never happened - would you? If you could start your life over, would you choose your mate?

Believe it or not, marriage/commitment is a choice that you make every day. You continue to make that choice until one day you question it... and, another day you decide to make a different choice.

If you cannot say, "YES! My mate are I are great together and we are happy with one another", then your relationship is in trouble. If you are not happier after years of marriage than you when you were wed, then you need help.

If you are asking yourself - "From Where We Started, How Did We Get Here?" - then the first place to look is your communication with your mate.

Where are You and Your Mate in Your Relationship - Right Now?

"The way we communicate with others and with ourselves ultimately determines the quality of our lives." (Anthony Robbins)

Do YOU Need This Book? Take a few minutes to take four tests. By the end of these tests, you will convince yourself... as to if/why you need this book.

1- *"Communication Rot"* Test:
   Is your communication with your mate rotten?

2- *"Stages of Kissing"* Test:
   What does kissing say about your relationship?

3- *"Trust Metrics"* Test:
   Can you trust your mate about what matters?

4- *"Trade Off"* Test:
   Are you better together with a mate or alone?

Before we start, ask yourself this question. *"The day before someone received a cancer diagnosis, were they really healthy?"* Of course, you will say *"No"* because their diagnosis only put an end to their ignorance about their problem.

That is what these communication tests will do for you... they will help you know, for sure, how healthy (or not) your relationship is.

1- Take this *"Communication Rot"* Test and see for yourself if communication between you and your mate needs improvement!

See how your relationship rates on these points of "rotten" communication:

1- **You feel afraid to ask for what you really want:** Before you even ask your mate for something, you are certain that you will be turned down, criticized, nit-picked, and generally misunderstood no matter what you say or do.

2- **You do not share your inner most thoughts:** You limit what you are willing to share with your mate from the start. You certainly will not share whatever makes you look vulnerable, uncertain, or weak with your partner.

3- **You feel criticized for whatever you do:** No matter what you say or do for your mate, you are made to feel that whatever you do or say is never good enough. Worse, you end up believing that it can never be good enough.

4- **You quarrel over topics not issues:** You focus on the small details (topics) and lose sight of the big picture (issues). By discussing what does not matter, you cannot resolve what does matter with your mate.

5- **You have the same argument repeatedly:** You are certain that however nice, kind, or polite you are to your mate, that this will end up in a fight... because you have had this same argument many times before.

6- **You feel pessimistic or hopeless:** You cannot envision communication with your mate having a positive result however much energy or effort you put into it. You are almost certain it will be a failure before you even start.

7- **You feel talk is pointless:** Even after you have discussed issues, you are certain that nothing significant will really change with your mate. At times, communication actually seems to make matters worse rather than better.

RESULT: If you and your mate believe one or more of the statements are true, then you need to improve your communication... before your relationship ends.

In a healthy relationship...
- You should be able to ask for what you want.
- You should be comfortable sharing your thoughts.
- You should feel comforted and not criticized.
- You should be able to discuss any topic openly.
- You should agree on solutions to your issues.
- You should be hopeful about keeping agreements.
- You should feel better after talking than before.

EXAMPLE: One woman who took this particular communication test realized that ALL of these statements were true of her marriage. She asked her husband to take this test and he agreed that their communication was rotten. Since they wanted to stay together, they immediately went on a marriage retreat to jump-start their communication. When they returned home, they went to marriage counseling to work on their issues. Their communication improved and so did their marriage.

2- Take this *"Stages of Kissing"* Test and see for yourself if communication between you and your mate needs improvement!

When, how, and how often couples kiss-hold hands are reliable indicators of the health of their relationship. Couples in love always WANT to kiss and hold hands, regardless of how long they have been together. They want the physical connection to their mate that is at the center of good romantic relationships.

See how your relationship rates on this scale of kissing and hand holding:

1 - You have kissed and held hands,
    it always was-is a rare occurrence.
        DISGUST: You are room-mates
    and you are like acquaintances.
        Outlook: You are divorced when it comes your romantic relationship.

2 - You have kissed and held hands but
    it was mainly only when dating.
        DISDAIN: You are room-mates
    and you are like cousins.
        Outlook: You are getting divorced in your romantic relationship.

3 - You enjoyed kissing and holding hands
    only when dating and newly married.
        DISLIKE: You are room-mates
    and you are like brother and sister.
        Outlook: You are heading towards divorce in your romantic relationship.

4 - You kissed and held hands a lot until
    you stopped due to having children.
        DISINTEREST: Your POOR communication is killing your relationship.

Outlook: Change in your communication might save your relationship.

5 - You kissed and held hands for a long time, but then it just stopped.
DISTANCE: Your relationship is POOR and your communication is POOR.
Outlook: Change in your communication could save your relationship.

6 - You kissed and held hands since dating, but it is on and off again.
PROPRIETY: Your romantic relationship and communication is OK.
Outlook: Change in your communication can create Pride.

7 - You kissed and held hands but it only happens at set and reliable times.
PRIDE: Your romantic relationship and communication is GOOD.
Outlook: Change in your communication can create Pleasure.

8 - You kissed and held hands and it happens fairly frequently when alone.
PLEASURE: Your romantic relationship and communication is GREAT.
Outlook: Change in your communication can create Passion.

9 - You kissed and held hands and it happens all the time no matter what.
PASSION: Your romantic relationship and communication is AWESOME.
Outlook: Your relationship will continue to be AWESOME for life.

RESULT: If you have rated your relationship kissing between 1 and 5, you and your mate are essentially unconnected and are likely to settle into boredom, wander into infidelity, or degenerate into divorce. If you have rated your relationship kissing between 6 and 9, you and your mate are connected and your relationship can be saved and improved by better communication.

EXAMPLE: Romantic touching is the icing on the cake of a relationship. Without kissing and touching, a relationship is more like brother and sister than husband and wife. One couple had a great marriage, except that the wife feared physical intimacy and had often refused it. She was shocked to discover that her husband had gone to a site for married people who wanted sex and nothing else. This broke her heart. She went for counseling to move past her fears of intimacy. Once she could act as a wife to her husband, he quit the dating site and it took their marriage to the next level.

3- Take this *"Trust Metrics"* Test and see for yourself if communication between you and your mate needs improvement!

See how your relationship rates on these points of trust in a romantic relationship:

1- **Honesty (90%):** *Is your mate is honest with you 90% of the time?* Even the closest of mates are going to have little secrets from one another, are going to tell little white lies, are going to forget things, or get them wrong... this should happen only 10% of the time. Mates who usually lie or do so quite often, kill their relationships because meaningful communication requires honesty.

2- **Openness (90%):** *Do you believe that you can tell your mate anything 90% of the time?* Just as honesty is the core of communication, openness is the foundation of all lasting relationships. If there is no openness more than 10% of the time, the relationship is bound to deteriorate and fail.

3- **Reliability (90%):** *Do you believe that you can rely on your mate 90% of the time?* The 10% of the time that you and your mate cannot trust one another should only be the times that you are working through your relationship issues. Reliability is created by honest communication and actions over an extended period. Where there can be no reliability, there is no relationship.

4- **Kindness (80%):** *Is your mate kind to you 80% of the time?* Modern life is so full of stress and activity that kindness is not always possible when times are challenging. Although mates should be kind to one another 100% of the time, the challenges of work, kids, finances, etc will strain relationships... but should not make them unkind. Where there is no kindness, there is no relationship.

5- **Harmony (80%):** *Do you feel harmony with your mate 80% of the time?* Harmony flows from kindness. Harmony is created by agreement on fundamentals: money, parenting, recreation, cleanliness, education, etc. Harmony is the oil that makes the relationship wheels run more smoothly.

6- **Investment (20%):** *Do you spend 20% of your time investing in making your relationship with your mate better?* If your romantic relationship is not good, start investing time in improving these relationship metrics!

RESULT: If you and your mate fall below these measures (metrics), then you will need to improve on them to save your relationship. All of these metrics depend upon good communication... that is why it is so essential to improve it.

EXAMPLE: One client laughed at the end of this test. This person said, *"I am not surprised... I do not trust my spouse as far as I could throw them!"* I asked, *"Then why are you married?"* This person fell silent on the phone. I remarked, *"It must be difficult to live with someone who you cannot trust..."* Not long after our talk, this individual's marriage broke up... over issues involving trust.

4- Take this *"Trade Off"* Test and see for yourself if communication between you and your mate needs improvement!

To be in a relationship, some things are gained while others are lost. Marriages succeed when they increase each partner's happiness. Marriages fail when one or both partners are unhappy in them. See how this trade off works for you:

1- *What do you feel most often in your relationship: love or obligation?* The best marriages are those between partners who love one another. If you view your marriage as an obligation or as a duty to your family, culture, or religion, then you need to improve your communication with your mate to get you back to the love you started your marriage with.

2- *Do you feel your partner supports you: physically, mentally, emotionally?* The vows of marriage - *"for better, for worse, for richer, for poorer, in sickness and in health"* - are for the *"help and support of each for the other."* If you and your partner are not supporting each other, then this is a poor trade-off.

3- *Do you feel your mate makes you feel attractive, loveable, sexy?* You and your partner should each be telling each other *"I love you"* each day. You both should feel loveable and sexy around one another. If you and your partner are not giving each other this kind of love, then this is a poor trade-off.

4- *Have you given up an important part of yourself for your relationship?* Marriage is always a trade-off. When marriages work, each mate gives up a little so they can gain a lot from being wed. Yet, if you or your partner have given up something important to be together, then this is a poor trade-off.

5- *Have you given up what you like to do, be, or have for your relationship?* If you have ever asked, "why do I have to give up myself to be loved by you?", then this is not only a poor trade-off, it is one that should never be made.

6- *Are you giving more than you are getting from your relationship?* Did you get married to become a money machine for your mate? Did you get married to become an unpaid domestic servant for your mate? These are poor trade-offs.

7- *Is there something you want from your partner that you are not getting?* Mates get married because each hopes that the other will bring something important to their life. Ask yourself: what was it that you most hoped to get out of your marriage? If you have not received it, then this is a poor trade-off.

8- *Does your partner have "rules for living" that you do not like?* Every mate has habits, preferences, and quirks that drive how they believe they "should" live. Often the two different sets of rules clash and create conflicts between mates. So if you are living with "bad" rules, then this is a poor trade-off.

9- *Do you kiss, hug, and/or make love out of love or out of obligation?* You and your partner should want to physically touch one another up to and including making love. If you cannot or do not want make love freely -or- if you are only being physically intimate out of duty, then this is a poor trade-off.

RESULT: If you or your mate gave unhappy answers to any of these questions, then the first step toward happiness is improving your communication. Start by asking for what you want and for what you have expected to receive.

EXAMPLE: One couple was experiencing great tension in their marriage. They went through this set of questions. One mate found that they were sick and tired of living by their partner's rules. The other mate revealed the one thing they needed from their partner that they were not getting. These discoveries helped them to make changes needed to continue on in their marriage.

<u>About These Tests</u>

If your relationship did not score very well on these tests, then you need to work on improving your communication with your mate - today!

You might be wondering where these tests are coming from. They come from 20 years of my experience in counseling clients about ways to improve their romantic relationships.

Yet, the only thing that matters is if this information helps you and your mate to improve both your communication and your romantic relationship!

What You Need to Know About Romantic Communication

Two Basic Human Needs in Communication

"To effectively communicate, we must realize that we are all different in the way we perceive the world and use this understanding as a guide to our communication with others." (Anthony Robbins)

The traditional definition of communication is "the exchange of information where one party (the sender) conveys a message to another (the receiver)." The main goals of communication are to:

- **Inform:** sender wants to give the receiver information about a topic.
- **Request:** sender wants to ask for the receiver to do/not do a specific action.
- **Persuade:** sender wants to change or reinforce the receiver's belief.
- **Good-will:** sender wants to build a relationship with the receiver.

While all of this is true, this does not explain WHAT makes communication work. What makes communication work can be summarized as **"Hear Me Because I Hear You!"** which taps into the TWO basic human needs:

NEED #1: "I desire to be heard and understood"
"The most basic of all human needs is the need to understand and be understood." (Ralph Nichols)

If you want to be HEARD (to be understood) then you must HEAR (to understand) what the other person is saying. Not only does that mean paying full attention to the other person, it means helping them to FEEL that you do hear them because you understand their point of view (where they are really coming from).

NEED #2: "I desire to be valued and respected"
"The deepest principle in human nature is the craving to be appreciated, valued, and respected." (William James)

If you want to be HEARD (to be valued and respected) then you must HEAR (showing that you value and respect) what the other person is saying. It means helping them to FEEL that you do hear them because you have their best interests at heart just as a friend would.

If you take nothing else from this book, remember these two needs. The vast majority of people will respond positively when you

GENUINELY hear, understand, value, and respect them (especially romantic partners).

EXAMPLE: A couple had a successful business because each of them had complimentary skills. One mate was a great sales person and the other was great at fulfillment. The problem was that each person did not truly value the other. The sales person said "If I did not bring in the sale, you would have nothing to make." The technician said, "If I could not make exactly what you promised, you would never be able to sell anything." Their marriage and their business were falling apart until they started hearing and respecting each other.

Three Part Romantic Communication Formula

"Being heard is so close to being loved that for the average person, they are almost indistinguishable." (David W. Augsburger)

Romantic Communication works on this formula:
Romantic Message = Verbal + Non-Verbal + Relationship Filter

If you and you mate are just not communicating effectively, then one or more parts in this romantic communication formula has broken down.

VERBAL: SPOKEN LANGUAGE (Auditory) (40%)
 Verbal = Words Spoken + Level of Voice + Tone of Voice

- **Words Spoken:** The words you speak matter! You will get a better response from your mate if the words you use are more logical, less emotional, and clearly state your viewpoint (instead of attacking your mate's viewpoint).

    Example: Compare these statements: which one is better?
1- *"You are WRONG about [fill in the blank]!"*
    This will shut down your partner's willingness to listen.
    This is an attack your partner must defend against.
2- *"I believe [fill in the blank] is not correct for [reason]."*
    This will encourage your partner to consider your words.
    This is only an invitation to consider your point of view.

- **Level of Voice:** This is when you (mainly) raise and (sometimes) lower your voice to emphasize points. THE LOUDER YOU SHOUT, the less your mate will listen to you. Make your points with logic and not BY SHOUTING.

    Example: Compare these statements: which one is better?
1- *"G-D IT! GET OVER HERE NOW AND [fill in the blank]!"*
    This will shut down your partner's

willingness to listen.
Many people will just walk away from such shouting.

2- *"I would like to sit down and talk about [fill in the blank]!"*
>This will encourage your partner to consider your words.
>This sets you both up for a productive discussion.

- **Tone of Voice:** This is when you change the softness or hardness in your voice to underline points. Hard voices express sarcasm, bitterness, and anger. The harder your voice is, the less your mate will listen to you. Soft voices express logic, rationality, and calmness. The softer your voice is, the more your mate will listen to you. Make your points with a calm, soft tone of voice.

>Example: Compare these statements: which one is better?

1- *"G-d it can you ever shut up and just listen to [fill in the blank]!"*
>This will shut down your partner's willingness to listen.
>Many people will just walk away from such anger.

2- *"Please hear me about [fill in the blank]!"*
>This will encourage your partner to consider your words.
>This sets you both up for a productive discussion.

NON-VERBAL: BODY LANGUAGE (Visual) (40%)
Non Verbal = Facial Expression + Hand Movements + Body Position

- **Facial Expression:** If you were being watched but the person watching could not hear you, and could only see your face, what would they conclude? Are your eyes full of love, hurt, or anger? Are your lips smiling or are they frowning? Faces will speak your mind more truthfully than any words you say.

    Example: Compare these statements: which one is better?
1- <u>You look away from your partner and say "[fill in the blank]!"</u>
    This will shut down your partner's willingness to listen.
    Many do not trust one who will not look them in the eye.
2- <u>You look your partner in the eye and say "[fill in the blank]!"</u>
    This will encourage your partner to consider your words.
    This sets you both up for a productive discussion.

- **Hand Movements:** If you were being watched but the person watching could not hear you, and could only see your hands, what would they conclude? Are your hands pointing toward you as if to draw your mate in? Are your hands pointing away from you as if to push your mate away? Hands will speak your mind more truthfully than any words you say.

    Example: Compare these hand expressions: which one is better?

1- <u>You cross your arms over your heart and say "[fill in the blank]!"</u>
    This will shut down your partner's willingness to listen.
    Many do not trust one who blocks their heart from view.

2- <u>You take your partner's hands in yours and say "[fill in the blank]!"</u>
    This will encourage your partner to consider your words.
    This sets you both up for a productive discussion.

- **Body Position:** If you were being watched but the person watching could not hear you, and could only see your body position, what would they conclude? Do you usually face or turn your back on your mate? Do you sit or stand close to your mate or do you move far away from them? When your mate comes near you, do you move closer to them or move farther away? Body position will speak your mind more truthfully than any words you say.

    Example: Compare these body positions: which one is better?

1- <u>You sit in a chair far from your mate and say "[fill in the blank]!"</u>

This will shut down your partner's willingness to listen.
Many do not trust one who distances themselves.

2- <u>You sit next to your mate, touching them, and say "[fill in the blank]!"</u>
This will encourage your partner to consider your words.
This sets you both up for a productive discussion.

NON-VERBAL: RELATIONSHIP FILTER (Kinesthetic) (20%)
Filter is Current Track Record of the Relationship Communication

- **Track Record:** This component of communication is the most important but the least discussed. This filter is the current state of you and your mate's track record with one another based upon all your past experience with them up to the present. This filter changes over time and falls into these categories.

1- *Overwhelmingly Positive:*
Your mate always does this: you love it.
2- *Borderline Positive:*
Your mate sometimes does this: you like it.
3- *Borderline Negative:*
Your mate sometimes does this: you dislike it.
4- *Overwhelmingly Negative:*
Your mate always does this: you hate it.

For every communication you have with your mate, you run it through this filter FIRST.

You run it through this filter BEFORE you react to the Verbal and Non-Verbal parts of your mate's communication. *The filter determines **how or if** you react to the Verbal and Non-Verbal parts of your mate's communication.*

Here is how the relationship filter works:

1- *Overwhelmingly Positive:*
> Your mate always does this: you love it. These are mates who are "as reliable as a clock" or "like money in the bank", etc. These mates do what they say and always keep their promises.
>
> When the relationship filter with your mate is "Overwhelmingly Positive", you become worried when your mate does not keep their promises... because they are so reliable. You are ready to believe their explanation of events.

2- *Borderline Positive:*
> Your mate sometimes does this: you like it.
>
> When the relationship filter with your mate is "Borderline Positive", you are willing to give your mate the benefit of the doubt when promises are broken. Yet, each time a promise is broken... the filter turns more negative.

3- *Borderline Negative:*
   Your mate sometimes does this: you dislike it.

   When the relationship filter with your mate is "Borderline Negative", you are not willing to give your mate the benefit of the doubt when promises are broken. Yet, each time a promise is broken... the filter turns even more negative.

4- *Overwhelmingly Negative:*
   Your mate always does this: you hate it.

   When the relationship filter is "Overwhelmingly Negative", any message will hit the filter, be rejected, and communication will break down.

If negative filters are not dealt with, they will shut down communication.

The goal of any communication improvement technique is to BREAK DOWN and CLEAR the negative filter BEFORE your romantic relationship is destroyed.

   Negative filters are associated with specific topics. For example: one mate asks another to pick up the kids at school. If one mate always comes up with excuses as to why they can never pick up the kids... the other mate will never believe them when they offer to do so. Track records speak louder than words.

So how do you identify the **EXACT blocks** created by negative filters? Easy, just answer the following questions - honestly - about your romantic relationship.

Identifying YOUR Relationship Issues Which BLOCK Communication

"We are all so desperate to be understood, we forget to be understanding." (Beau Taplin)

Unresolved relationship issues are the reasons WHY the communication between you and your mate is not good. If you want to improve your communication with your partner, then both of you must answer the following questions - honestly. Each NO answer is a block in YOUR relationship that needs to be healed... as soon as possible.

NOTE: *If one mate refuses to answer these questions, the relationship is over.*

Lasting Relationships: Key #1 - Friendship

"Love is friendship that has caught fire. It is quiet understanding, mutual confidence, sharing and forgiving. It is loyalty through good and bad times. It settles for less than perfection and [it] makes allowances for human weaknesses." (Ann Landers)

Genuine friendship between loving partners is the rock upon which love endures and passion keeps burning ever more brightly. Friendship depends on solid communication. Before your mate is anything else... they should be your friend.

If you and your mate want a lasting relationship, it begins and ends with each of you being the best friend to one another... that "truest, dearest, and tenderest" friend. If you and your mate want to work on one thing to keep you together - apart from communication - that thing should be friendship.

To have a friend in your mate, you need to be a friend to your mate. Could both you and your partner answer "Yes" - with total honesty - to all of the following questions in this "Friendship Test"?

* Do you genuinely enjoy...
    - spending time (talking, recreation) with your mate (apart from sex)?
    - being in the company (physical presence) of your mate (apart from sex)?
* Do you feel safe, loved, and protected... (physically, mentally, and emotionally) by your mate?
* Do you feel that you can trust your mate...
    - with truth (keeping your secrets and being trustworthy)?
    - with money (not stealing from you or bankrupting you)?
    - with fidelity (not cheating on you with others)?

* Do you value and respect your mate's... opinions, judgments, and beliefs (taking them seriously)?
* All things being equal, would you rather be with your mate... than anyone else (apart from being in bed)?
* If you were suddenly injured, would your mate be... the first person you would call on for help?
* If you were seriously troubled about something... would your mate be the first person you would tell?
* If you were laying on your deathbed and could call someone... would it be your mate?
* Is your mate your best friend (apart from sex)... because they truly have your best interests at heart?

If both you and your mate have answered "Yes" to all of the above questions, then - congratulations! - you are indeed best friends. Wherever you or your mate have answered "No", you have surfaced an issue between you. It is one that you will need to resolve if you want to make your relationship last.

EXAMPLE: When one couple took this test, the husband was astonished to learn that his wife thought that he NEVER took her seriously. He had much more formal education than she did. He was constantly bringing up his "superior" knowledge of whatever they were talking about and often said to her *"case closed"* ending the discussion. After taking this test, she said, *"If you cannot start taking me seriously, I am done with you - case closed"* and he was shocked. So, the husband changed his ways and they stayed married.

<u>Lasting Relationships: Key #2 - Understanding</u>

"To understand and to be understood makes our happiness." (Proverb)

To be a friend, each must work on "understanding where the other is coming from." Could both you and your partner answer "Yes" - with total honesty - to all of the following questions in this "Understanding Test"?

> * Do you sincerely believe that your mate... has your best interests at heart (unconditional love)?
> * Do you feel that your mate understands...
>   - the stresses and pressures that you are dealing with?
>   - and values your contribution to the relationship?
>   - that you value their contribution to the relationship?
>   - and listens to, respects, and values your opinions and beliefs?
>   - sees, pays attention to, and responds to your feelings?

- your point of view about your family (parents/siblings)?
- your point of view about your children (discipline, etc)?
- your point of view about spending money (priorities)?
- your point of view about your career (versus family life)?
- your needs, wants, and desires as a loving being?
- that you value their needs, wants, and desires?

If both you and your mate has answered "Yes" to all of the above questions, then - congratulations! - you are "on the same page." Wherever you or your mate have answered "No", you have surfaced an issue between you.

Resolving misunderstandings are especially critical if you truly want to make your relationship last. For it is long term unresolved misunderstandings that will erode the basis of the most solid friendships.

EXAMPLE: When a couple took this test, the wife was surprised to learn that her husband was completely stressed out over her attitude toward money. They both worked and they had "plenty saved" in her eyes... but not in his. He had grown up poor and had to constantly do without. For him, money was for safety (as in having it in the bank) and for her, money was for achieving goals (as in spending it). So, they compromised. They agreed on the amount of savings ("never to be touched") and on what goals money would be spent on.

Lasting Relationships: Key #3 - Honesty

"Honesty is the fastest way to prevent a mistake from turning into a failure." (James Altucher)

To be a friend, each mate must commit themselves to being totally honest with one another. Could both you and your partner answer "Yes" - with total honesty - to all of the following questions in this "Honesty Test"?

* Do you sincerely believe that your mate...
  - genuinely wants to be honest with you
    (not lie)?
  - always is telling you the truth
    (to the best of their ability)?
  - is honest about how they spend money
    (no secret funds)?
  - is honest about how they spend their time
    (when apart)?
  - has been honest about their past
    (former lovers, etc)?
  - has been faithful to you
    (not sleeping with exes, etc)?
  - is honest with your children
    (supporting your decisions)?
  - is honest with your family
    (not undermining you)?

- is honest with your friends (delivering messages, etc)?
- is honest about health choices (smoking, drinking, etc)?
- is honest about lifestyle choices (gambling, gaming, etc)?
- is honest about recovery (working to break addictions, etc)?

If both you and your mate have answered "Yes" to all of the above questions, then - congratulations! - you have developed a healthy bond of honesty. Wherever you or your mate have answered "No", you have surfaced an issue between you. Without honesty, you and your mate cannot improve your communication and create a lasting relationship.

EXAMPLE: When a couple took this test, the husband had not realized how threatened his second wife was over his dealings with his first wife. He and his first wife had a "special needs" child who would throw tantrums if his father did not come around often. So, the husband and the first wife were together more than the second wife liked. There was a simple solution: the second wife went with her husband to tend to the child when needed which resolved the conflict.

Lasting Relationships: Key #4 - Love

"There is only one happiness in this life, to love and be loved." (George Sand)

To be a friend, each mate must love the partner for their unique qualities (apart from bed). Could both you and your partner answer "Yes" - with total honesty - to all of the following questions in this "Love Test"?

* Do you feel that your mate loves you regardless of...
    - your looks (if you are not good looking)?
    - your weight (if you are too thin or too fat)?
    - your physical health (disabilities, handicaps)?
    - your mental health (hang ups, phobias)?
    - your emotional health (anger, withdrawal)?
    - your religious beliefs (dismissive)?
    - your education (if you are less educated)?
    - your background (if not the same as theirs)?
    - your work situation (at time of conflicts)?
    - your habits and quirks (that annoy them)?
    - your struggles (with addictions, problems)?
    - their family's criticisms (about you)?

If both you and your mate have answered "Yes" to all of the above questions, then - congratulations! - your love is very grounded in genuine mutual attraction, affection, admiration, and acceptance. Wherever you or your mate have answered "No", you have surfaced an issue between you.

Love is the glue that holds a relationship together. For only love can get you and your mate through the "rough spots" that all couples face. "Love will keep you together" as long as you remain friends.

EXAMPLE: I will use myself here. I was born with disabilities in my physical health which made me less available to my husband than a wife would normally be. This broke up our marriage. I often think if I had asked my ex-husband all these questions before we married, this would have saved us both heartbreak of divorce.

Lasting Relationships: Key #5 - Openness
"If you keep an open mind, you can learn so much from the people around you." (Lynn Good)

To be a friend, each mate must feel comfortable enough to be entirely open with one another. Could both you and your partner answer "Yes" - with total honesty - to all of the following questions in this "Openness Test"?

* Do you feel comfortable that your mate does their best...
  - to keep you physically safe (protected)?
  - to support you mentally (no criticisms)?
  - to nurture you emotionally (dries your tears)?
* Do you feel comfortable and relaxed in your mate's presence
  (like you can let your hair down)?
* Do you feel comfortable
  - in revealing your innermost thoughts to your mate (no fear of rejection)?
  - in bouncing ideas off your mate

    (they will not ridicule or criticize you)?
- that your mate will keep your confidences
  (not tell their friends, etc)?
- to risk failing in front of your mate
  (they will understand)?
- to risk being foolish in front of your mate
  (they will accept it)?
- to risk being vulnerable to your mate
  (they will not hurt you)?
- that your mate does not hold things back
  (or hide things)?
- that you do not have to hold things back
  (or hide things)?

If both you and your mate have answered "Yes" to all of the above questions, then - congratulations! - you are comfortable with one another. Wherever you or your mate have answered "No", you have surfaced an issue between you.

Lasting relationships can only exist where both partners are fundamentally comfortable with one another. It is very difficult to communicate with or spend lots of time happily with someone who makes you uncomfortable in your daily life.

EXAMPLE: When a couple took this test, the wife blurted out to her husband that "I feel like I am always on trial with you" (the husband was an attorney). She felt, at times, like he was examining her as if she was in a court room under oath. He was unaware that he was treating her this way. He asked her what specifically it was that he said and did to make her feel that way. She gave him very precise details and he stopped his "lawyer-like" behavior with her at once.

Lasting Relationships: Key #6 - Sharing

"When two hearts as one unite, sorrow is not heavy and the burden is made light." (Amish Proverb)

To be a friend, each mate must feel they are in a partnership based on equal sharing. Could both you and your partner answer "Yes" - with honesty - to all of the following questions in this "Sharing Test"?

* Does your mate share with you, relatively equally...
  - responsibility for money earning (outside jobs)?
  - decisions about spending big money (cars, furniture, etc)?
  - decisions about spending small money (food, clothes, etc)?
  - decisions about recreational time (travel, vacation, etc)?
  - household chores (especially unpleasant tasks)?
  - planning special events (birthday parties, etc)?
  - dealing with family conflicts (children, in-laws, etc)?

- resolving marital arguments (compromising)?
- resolving work conflicts (managing schedules)?
- disciplining children (telling them "no")?
- handling children (driving them, seeing teachers, etc)?
- dealing with healthcare (doctor's visits, etc)?

If both you and your mate have answered "Yes" to all of the above questions, then - congratulations! - you have a sharing, caring partnership. Wherever you or your mate have answered "No", you have surfaced an issue between you.

Lasting relationships can only exist where both partners are willing to share all of who they are and all of what they have with one another. Sharing with your partner shows you care for them. When you care, communication is easy.

EXAMPLE: When a couple took this test, the husband had not realized how much it bothered him when his wife shared details about "his private business" with others. These were not state secrets and these were details that most people would have been willing to share... but not him. That his wife was "over-sharing" was undermining his trust in her. So, she agreed not to share anything about her husband... unless he first gave his permission to do so. That ended up eliminating much of the tension that was in their marriage.

Lasting Relationships: Key #7 - Loving
"When my lips meet thine, Thy very soul is wedded unto mine." (H. H. Boyesen)

To be a friend and lover in bed, each must feel that their personal needs, wants, and desires are being met. Could both you and your partner answer "Yes" - with total honesty - to all of the following questions in this "Loving Test"?

* While having sex, do you and your mate...
  - share initiating loving contact (equally)?
  - both show affection by kissing one another (before/after)?
  - both show affection by hugging one another (before/after)?
  - both act like you desire one another's bodies (both feeling desired)?
  - share decisions about loving practices (doing only what both like)?
  - exchange words of love (instead of just "doing it" to one another)?
  - share responsibility for arousal (turning each other on in loving)?
  - share responsibility for mutual happiness (each getting satisfied)?
  - share quality time in the After Glow (not just sleeping right after)?
  - attend to each other's personal needs, wants, and desires (caring)?
  - both always feel comfortable with what goes on (no force, no harm)?

If both you and your mate have answered "Yes" to all of the above questions, then you have a lifetime of great loving to look forward to. Wherever you or your mate have answered "No", you have surfaced an issue between you.

Loving is what makes lasting relationships truly wonderful. For super satisfying closeness can only be shared between those mates who are the best of friends and the tenderest of lovers. Loving is the ultimate form of communication.

EXAMPLE: When a couple took this test, the wife told her husband that their loving was so unsatisfying to her... that she did not want to answer this set of questions. He pointed out that things could not get better unless she did. It turned out that the husband was a very high energy person. He was always jumping from thing to thing, including lovemaking. The solution became for him to commit to a certain block of time in bed with her. After a while, he found that he enjoyed taking things slower for a while... and their loving improved.

Common Sources of Relationship Conflict

"Looking back and wondering if it could have worked eventually hurts more than trying and failing." (Dominic Riccitello)

<u>**One final test:**</u> <u>What are the main sources of conflict with your mate?</u>

Here are the primary sources of relationship conflicts which lead to divorce.

1> **Communication:** The key reason for divorce is failure of communication. Prime candidates for divorce are: those couples who have stopped talking, who communicate only on trivial and necessary matters, or who cannot say anything good about one another. When spouses are unwilling to share what is really going inside their minds and hearts, they are already divorced. It is only by honest and meaningful communication that the other problems can be solved.

2> **Money/Work:** Prime candidates for divorce are: those couples who cannot agree on saving and spending priorities, who cannot agree on how much time is devoted to work and recreation, or who do not contribute equally to the marriage in terms of earning money or in terms of the completion of household tasks or being helpful in general.

3> **Parenting:** Prime candidates for divorce are: those couples who cannot agree on parenting priorities, methods, and discipline, who always put their child(ren) and/or relatives before their spouse, or who abdicate their parental responsibilities.

4> **Sex/Infidelity:** Prime candidates for divorce are: those couples who have ceased to have relations, who find sex unsatisfying, who are unfaithful, who contract STDs, or who cannot agree on sex at all.

5> **Cleanliness:** Prime candidates for divorce are: those couples who cannot agree on their mutual personal hygiene, on the level of organization of their shared living space, or who have "let themselves go" physically.

6> **Relatives:** Prime candidates for divorce are: those couples who deeply dislike one another's birth families, who feel that relatives interfere too much in their marriage, or who feel that interactions with relatives are inappropriate.

7> **Incapacity:** Prime candidates for divorce are: those couples where one of the partners/children has been born with or has acquired a permanent physical-mental-emotional incapacity whether through illness, injury, or accident.

8> **Addictions:** Prime candidates for divorce are: those couples where one of the partners/children has developed addictions (like alcohol, drugs, gambling, porno, pageants, games, etc) that strain the family's financial resources.

9> **Tragedy:** Prime candidates for divorce are: those couples who have experienced a major tragedy like violent crime, the death of a child, prolonged hospitalization, lengthy court trial, or costly dispute with the government.

10> **Expectations/Priorities:** Prime candidates for divorce are: partners who stop being committed to the marriage because one undergoes a dramatic change in priorities, because one fails to live up to pre-marital promises, or because one discovers that their marriage is based on lies told by the other.

11> **No Trust/Boredom:** Prime candidates for divorce are: partners who no longer love, trust, or appreciate their mate and/or one mate who is tired of their partner's selfishness, constant criticism, cruelty, and/or non-stop anger.

12> **Change Makers:** Prime candidates for divorce are: mates who have tried and failed to "mold" their partner as they wished to, mates who have changed what they want out of life, and/or mates who have outgrown one another.

Part 2: How to Improve Communication in Your Relationship

Love, Honor, and Cherish Through Better Communication

"Two monologues do not make a dialogue."
(Jeff Daly)

"Love, honor, and cherish"... those are easy words to say when exchanging wedding vows. They are a lot harder to stick to in real life... because real life creates real conflicts. For those who claim to be in the 1% of all couples who never "fight", understand that there is only one cause of the "no fight" union:

* If one partner always gives into the other, then master and slave are in agreement and there are no fights.

99% of people (myself included) do not fit into that 1% category. 99% of people live in the real world of unresolved issues end relationships. That is the bad news. The good news is that conflict does not have to end a loving union... If conflict is managed properly it can increased the unity of a couple:

* If partners chose not to view their interaction as "fights" but rather as "discussions, negotiations, conferences", this will increase closeness inside their relationship.

How to Get the Most Out of This Book

The most important tool in this book is the "AAA Technique to Create A+ Relationships" and that tool should be mastered first. If you need to quickly start improving your communication with your mate, then start sending your mate *romantic text messages* to get positive communication flowing.

There are many tools in this book. You do not need to use them all at once. Some tools will appeal to you and your mate while others will not. You and your mate should agree on which tools are best for improving your relationship.

Before we start on them, there are a few common misconceptions about communication in romantic relationships which must be cleared up first.

Misconceptions About Romantic Relationships

"I love you more because I believe you had liked me for my own sake and for nothing else." (John Keats)

If you or your mate believe any of the following, then your romantic relationship is in trouble. These are common misconceptions... that many believe are true. If you want to improve your communication with your mate, get rid of them:

1- **Happily Ever After:** Mates who believe in the myth of *"happily ever after"* (as depicted in romance novels) are headed for trouble. Relationships are always changing because life is always changing. Relationships which last and endure are based on commitment, which develops and deepens as mates work together to meet life's challenges.

2- **You Complete Me:** Mates who have unrealistic expectations of what it means to have a partner are sabotaging their relationship from the start. Good relationships are between two whole people who are joining their lives and not between two "half" people who are struggling to become "one" person.

3- **Mind Reading:** Mates who think things like *"if you love me, then you will know what I want without* me asking" and "if we are meant to be together then we will be" are headed for trouble. Mates cannot read each other minds. If there is something "wrong" in your relationship, then it is up to both of you to speak up and share your thoughts.

4- **Papering Over the Cracks:** Mates who rely on things like *"I will just have mind blowing sex with my mate and all will be well"* or *"another child will keep our marriage together"* or *"I will give my mate a cool gift and they will calm down"* are living in fantasy land. These kinds of quick fixes never ever last.

4- **Losing the Spark:** Mates who regard the "romantic spark" as the only measure of success in their relationship are sabotaging it. Over time, the initial spark should turn into a deep flame. The relationship inside the bedroom can only be as good as the relationship outside of it. If you and your mate have lost your spark, start building your flame by improving your communication.

6- **Letting Outsiders In:** Mates who complain to outsiders (like family and friends) about their partner are setting up their relationship for failure. Family and friends will take sides and this will just increase the conflict between mates. Keeping problems only between mates creates the space to solve them.

7- **Jealousy is Caring:** Mates who are jealous of one another are not showing how much they care. Jealous mates are actually showing their partner just how insecure they are about themselves and about the relationship in general. The jealous mate should handle their insecurity before it damages their romantic relationship.

8- **Fighting is Failure:** Mates, who consider that "fighting is failure" and avoid it at all costs, have shut down their communication. Mates, who avoid certain topics, just keep taboo problems from being solved. Everything should be open for discussion. Counselors can help mates resolve problems that they cannot solve by themselves. Getting help is not failure: it is a chance for success.

About the Impossible Double Bind

"Cause other people to like themselves just a little bit better and I'll promise you this they will like you very much." (Chesterfield)

Mates in a romantic relationship almost always have experienced the "double bind" phenomenon. This is best explained by an example. Without being told, one mate "just knows" there is something bothering their partner. When they ask "what is wrong?" and their partner says "nothing", the mate who asked knows this to be untrue. Later the partner may end up confessing the problem.

How does this work? When mates speak, they notice their partner's reaction (how they look and what they say) but they also feel the energy from their heart. When the partner's words and actions (from their mind) do not match this energetic emotional feeling (from their heart), their mate is sure to notice this disconnection.

If you want your mate to really hear you, you must mean what you say and say what you mean. This is the only way to avoid the double bind of your words saying one thing and your energy saying another.

To get others, especially your mate, to hear you, then your words and body language must match your thoughts and feelings. **Your mate will know when these do not match.**

Double binds only accomplish one thing: destroying trust in a romantic relationship.

Myths of Conflict Romantic Resolution

"Seek first to understand, then to be understood." (Stephen R. Covey)

When two individuals join their lives together, there are bound to be differences of opinion that must be resolved. To do this, the following myths of conflict resolution must be exploded first.

* **MYTH #1:** *Love Means Never Having to Say You are Sorry:* Bunk! Love means both having to say they are sorry quite often... and to mean it. Human beings are born to make mistakes and to learn from

them. Unwillingness to admit mistakes, wrongs, errors, or faults just keeps the conflict alive and keeps mates locked into opposing war-like positions. The willingness to say sorry opens the doors to resolving conflict for good and help unblock relationship communication.

* **MYTH #2:** *Increasing the Conflict - "I'm Right!":* So what? Your mate thinks they are right. It is very likely that you are right about some issues and your mate is right about others. Conflict can drag on because one or both partners need to be right and that outweighs every other consideration (like love, happiness, common sense, etc). Being right is not what ends conflicts. What ends them is consensus and compromise which unblocks communication.

* **MYTH #3:** *Avoiding the Conflict - Withdrawal:* Happier being alone? When one or both partners choose to avoid the conflict, they end up avoiding one another. Conflict does not go away if it is ignored: it just comes out in other forms until it is so gigantic that it can no longer be pushed to the side. By that time, the romantic relationship is "on the respirator" and one of them will pull the plug unless drastic measures are taken to unblock their communication and get it going again.

* **MYTH #4:** *Conflicts Will Resolve Themselves:* Love does not automatically solve all problems. Good marriages do not come naturally. They require work by both partners in overcoming the

challenges that life sends everyone. This book has many tools to help do this: if only you will pick them up and use them to heal your relationship.

Overview of Tools for Better Communication

"It is the province of knowledge to speak and it is the privilege of wisdom to listen." (Oliver Wendell Holmes)

Conflict can be like a heart attack in the romantic relationship... and it will only survive so many. The best strategy in communicating with your mate is to work in partnership with them so that conflict is minimized and love is maximized:

* **Loving Feedback:** Conflict can be resolved by using the *"AAA Technique to Create A+ Relationships."* This technique has been used successfully by couples for many years to give "loving feedback" to one another... instead of arguing. Unless you enjoy arguing (which some people do), this technique can stop small differences from blowing up into big problems.

* **Learning to "Fight Fair":** "Fair Fighting" means both partners stay focused on the common goal of creating mutually satisfying solutions to issues. This focus is achieved when both mates commit to "fair" practices like complaining without belittling one another and criticizing without cataloging past sins.

* **Making Decisions Together:** Nothing demonstrates commitment between mates more than their working in partnership to make decisions together based on consensus and reached through compromise. By the "give and take" in their joint decisions, mates develop the cooperation necessary in sustaining lasting relationships. Communication is the KEY to making great decisions.

* **Giving/Receiving Forgiveness:** The best way mates can unblock their communication is by giving and receiving forgiveness. Mates must forgive themselves their faults and forgive faults in their mates. By learning to curb the desire to keep score as well as to cultivate calmness and flexibility, both partners will be able to give and receive forgiveness. This will go a long way to improving communication and centering their relationship in harmony and love.

* **Loving Communication:** Conflict partly results from unloving communication. When mates work on developing more loving communication - focusing on compassion, courtesy, and compliments - they create more harmony in their lives and they increase their level of intimacy... which leads to great loving!

The Master Communication Formula

Loving Feedback: The AAA Technique to Create A+++ Relationships

"The greatest compliment that was ever paid me

was when one asked me what I thought, and attended to my answer." (Henry David Thoreau)

If you feel like your mate is just "not listening to you" or you are "not getting your point of view" across, then this **"Structured Feedback Approach"** will definitely help you. It is easier than it looks... and more to the point... it works!

<u>AAA: Accuracy, Agreement, and Action.</u>

For the best results with AAA, do no more than 3 issues in 30 minutes each day. This AAA technique works only if you and your mate work it.

1- **Accuracy** and honesty are the keys to making this structured approach to feedback work. Ex. *"one mate is always working late."*

- **State the problem:** start by using the "I" word as in "I feel..." or "I think..." or I believe..." Ex. *"I feel you are neglecting me when you come home late."*

- **Use specific details:** continue by saying "I feel sad when you... said, did, forgot to do..." Ex. *"Last Tuesday I cooked your favorite meal. After it was ready, you texted to say you would be so late that I should eat without you."*

- **Encourage exploration:** end by asking "What do you feel-think about this?" and start discussing it. Ex. *"I feel sad and upset when you do not eat with* *me. I feel like you no longer value our relationship... or even like me (let alone love me) anymore."*

2- **Agreement** is the goal of this structured approach to feedback: move from words to actions. Ex. *"How to have boundaries between home and work in a way that serves us both?"*

- **Summarize the problem:** each person says what they think the problem is from their viewpoint. Ex. *"I feel like I must stay late at work or risk losing my job"* and the reply is *"I feel like you value the job more than you value me."*

- **Explore feelings:** each person shares their thoughts, feelings, and ideas about the problem. Ex. *"I think it is important that we spend more time together"* and the reply is *"I agree but I am not sure how that is going to work."*

- **Identify differences:** both people agree on where the points of disagreement are, what the problem is. Ex. *"Maybe you getting a less demanding job - where you would be home on time - would help us to spend more time together?"* and the reply is *"I really like my job and I do not want to change it."*

- **Reach agreement:** both people agree that they genuinely want to work together to solve the problem. Ex. *"We agree that my work is keeping us from spending enough time. Jobs come and go but our relationship is what matters."*

3- **Action** is the result of this structured approach to feedback: to create actions that solve the problems. Ex. *"Since dinners cannot always work out, let us meet for lunch on a regular basis. Meeting for lunch would work like this..."*

- **State desired outcome:** both people state how they would like the problem to be solved. Ex: *"We will meet for lunch each Tuesday."*

- **Pick from alternatives:** both people offer, discuss, and then pick from among alternative solutions. Ex. *"I will text you if Tuesday just cannot work for lunch because things just come up."*

- **Determine evaluation:** both people agree on measures of success (how will we know that it works?) Ex. *"If a Tuesday lunch cannot work because of an emergency, then we will definitely meet for lunch two days later on Thursday."*

- **Schedule follow up:** both people set a time to see if their agreement is working or if it needs changing. Ex. *"For the last four weeks, we have eaten lunch together at least once a week and it has helped our relationship!"*

Example: Resolving MONEY Conflicts

Conflicts about money are most often about driven by fear and power. Money is power. Fear arises in one mate when the actions or inactions of their partner seem to or do threaten their financial security in the future. These differences in the use and purpose of money are bound to create conflicts.

1- **Lack of Security:** You fear that you will not have any financial security in your future because of the actions or inactions of your mate.

2- **Lack of Control:** You fear that you will lose control over the quality of your life because of the financial actions or inactions of your mate.

3- **Lack of Approval:** You fear that others you care for will disapprove of you or disrespect you if you cannot maintain a certain level of finances.

4- **Lack of Priority:** You fear that you will not realize your dreams and/or be able to have control over the issues impacting your life due to lack of money.

If you and your mate have conflicts over money, look for the fears attached to it. These are key to getting to the bottom of your money issues.

1- **Accuracy** and honesty are the keys to this structured approach to feedback.

- **State the problem:**
  Start by using the "I" word as in "I feel..." or "I think..." or I believe..."

Mate 1: *"I feel like we are not saving enough money. I fear that if we do not start saving more or spending less then we will not have money for everything we have planned, like getting the roof repaired."*

Mate 2: *"You are worrying too much. When we need to replace the roof, we will have the money. You always think there will never be enough."*

- **Use specific details:**
  Continue by saying "I feel sad when you...
      said, did, forgot to do..."

Mate 1: *"I am so worried. Please take a look at this spreadsheet. I have projected what it will cost and what we can earn. When you do the math, you will see that we will not have enough to repair the roof when the time comes."*

Mate 2: *"I am not worried. Right now, we can get a few more years out of the roof. You are not taking into accounts the raises we will get."*

- **Encourage exploration:**
  End by asking "What do you feel-think about this?"
      and start discussing it.

Mate 1: *"I feel terribly worried that if we put off repairing the roof we will cause damage to the house which will cost us more to fix in the end."*

Mate 2: *"I feel that we cannot lives our lives based on worrying about what will or will not happen with money in the future. Our house will be fine for now."*

2- **Agreement** is the goal of feedback is to move from words to actions.

- **Summarize the problem:**
  Each says what they think the problem is from their viewpoint.

Mate 1: *"I feel like you are not listening to me. I feel like we will wake up one day to find the roof leaking water on us. I just do not want to live like that."*

Mate 2: *"I feel like you are not listening to me. I feel like we have more time to save up for the roof. I want to have some fun for a change."*

- **Explore feelings:**
  Each shares their thoughts, feelings, and ideas about the problem.

Mate 1: *"I feel like we are not being responsible with our money."*
Mate 2: *"I feel like we are being trapped by fears about money."*

- **Identify differences:**
  Both agree on where the points of disagreement are, what the problem is.

Mate 1: *"I feel like we should have already repaired the roof."*
Mate 2: *"I know that we need to repair the roof... just not now."*

- **Reach agreement:**
  Both agree that they genuinely want to
      work together to solve the problem.

Mate 1: *"I want to agree on a date when we will repair the roof."*
Mate 2: *"I want us to agree that we do not have to do it right now."*

3- **Action** is the result of feedback: to create
      actions that solve the problems.

- **State desired outcome:**
  Both state how they would like the
      problem to be solved.

Mate 1: *"I feel we should start looking into options to repair the roof."*
Mate 2: *"I feel we should get a contractor's opinion about a repair."*

- **Pick from alternatives:**
  Both offer, discuss, and then pick from
      among alternative solutions.

Mate 1: *"I agree to getting an opinion about when to repair the roof."*

Mate 2: *"I agree to get the repair when the contractor says so."*

- **Determine evaluation:**
  Both agree on measures of success
    (how will we know that it works?)

Mate 1: *"I will get the first opinion on the roof today."*
Mate 2: *"I will get the second opinion on the roof the following week."*

- **Schedule follow up:**
  Both set a time to see if their agreement is working
    or if it needs changing.

The mates agree to their action plan. When both contractors agree that the roof should be repaired, the mates agree upon a date for that work to be completed.

Example: Resolving PARENTING Conflicts

Conflicts about parenting most often have their origins in the mates' childhoods. More often than not, each mate has been parented in a different way. Each mate has emerged from their birth family with different beliefs about how parenting is best done. These differences are will create conflicts.

1- **Allowance:** You believe that your children should get an allowance (letting them relax) or have to work for their money (building their character).

2- **Education:** You believe that your children are receiving too little education (are unprepared) or too much education (stressing them out).

3- **Chores:** You believe that your children are doing too little (not learning to be self sufficient) or too many chores (being treated like unpaid employees).

4- **Discipline:** You believe that your children are being disciplined too strictly (not having fun) or not strictly enough (teaching them to be lazy).

If you and your mate have conflicts over parenting, look for differences in these styles. These are key to getting to the bottom of your parenting issues.

1- **<u>Accuracy</u>** and honesty are the keys to this structured approach to feedback.

- **State the problem:**
   Start by using the "I" word as in "I feel..."
   or "I think..." or I believe..."

Mate 1: *"I feel as if you are too easy on our daughter because you favor her."*
Mate 2: *"I feel as if you are too easy on our son because you favor him."*

- **Use specific details:**
   Continue by saying "I feel sad when you...
   said, did, forgot to do..."

Mate 1: *"I feel that you are too easy on our daughter because you allowed her to use her phone even though we agreed that she was still grounded."*

Mate 2: *"I feel that you are too easy on our son because you allowed him to play sports even though we agreed that he should have been studying."*

- **Encourage exploration:**
  End by asking "What do you feel-think about this?" and start discussing it.

Mate 1: *"I think you favor our daughter because she looks like your late mother and you still miss your mother. I think this is why you favor her."*

Mate 2: *"I think you favor our son because you only had brothers growing up and you are not used to female children. I think this is why you favor him."*

2- **Agreement** is the goal of feedback is
    to move from words to actions.

- **Summarize the problem:**
  Each says what they think the problem
      is from their viewpoint.

Mate 1: *"It is not good for parents to favor one child over another."*
Mate 2: *"Our favoritism is causing our children to fight needlessly."*

- **Explore feelings:**
  Each shares their thoughts, feelings, and ideas about the problem.

Mate 1: *"Our daughter spends far too much time on the phone. She will text and chat all day if we do not set limits. She risks not getting into college."*

Mate 2: *"Our son needs to study more. If we allow him to play sports all the time, he will never earn grades good enough to get into college."*

- **Identify differences:**
  Both agree on where the points of disagreement are, what the problem is.

Mate 1: *"Our son cannot study all day. He needs time for sports."*
Mate 2: *"Our daughter cannot study all day. She needs time for friends."*

- **Reach agreement:**
  Both agree that they genuinely want to work together to solve the problem.

Mate 1: *"We should give our children better guidelines over how they spend their time."*
Mate 2: *"As parents, we must treat both our children equally. Favoritism in bad for a family."*

3- **Action** is the result of feedback: to create actions that solve the problems.

- **State desired outcome:**
  Both state how they would like the
    problem to be solved.

Mate 1: *"We need to have rules that apply to both children equally."*
Mate 2: *"We need to enforce those rules to both children equally."*

- **Pick from alternatives:**
  Both offer, discuss, and then pick from
    among alternative solutions.

Mate 1: *"I will give our daughter time alone on the phone while you are out with our son. When she finishes, I will ask her how it went so we can bond."*

Mate 2: *"I will drive our son to sports. I will see that he arrives and leaves on schedule. While we drive home, I will ask about his studies so we can bond."*

- **Determine evaluation:**
  Both agree on measures of success
    (how will we know that it works?)

The mates agree to a block of time when they split up so that their children can do their separate activities. They agree that their children will lose their privileges (phone time or sports practice) if they fail to keep up their grades.

- **Schedule follow up:**
  Both set a time to see if their agreement is working or if it needs changing.

The mates agree to try their new system for a month and see how it works for them. They see what changes they can make to make the process better.

Example: Resolving INTIMACY Conflicts

Conflicts about sexual intimacy are among the hardest to resolve. Sex is not just about relating to your partner. It is about the sexual attitudes that each mate learned from their birth family, their friends, their school, and society. These differences in outlook and upbringing will heavily influence how each mate relates to the other during sex. This is bound to create conflicts.

1- **Mismatched:** You believe your mate wants to make love too much or not enough. Rarely are mates equal in their desire for physical intimacy.

2- **Expectations:** You believe sex must always result in climax or that, as long as touching is satisfying to both, climax is not always needed.

3- **Issues:** You believe it is better to resolve issues before making love or it is better to make love, even if angry, because it is good for the relationship.

4- **Timing:** You believe it is much better to be spontaneous (love when the mood strikes you) or it is better to be planned (preparation makes perfect).

If you and your mate have conflicts over sex, look for differences in these needs. These are key to getting to the bottom of your intimacy issues.

1- **<u>Accuracy</u>** and honesty are the keys to this structured approach to feedback.

- **State the problem:**
  Start by using the "I" word as in "I feel..." or "I think..." or I believe..."

Mate 1: *"I feel like you want to have sex too often. It tires me out."*
Mate 2: *"I feel like you hardly ever want to have sex. It frustrates me."*

- **Use specific details:**
  Continue by saying "I feel sad when you... said, did, forgot to do..."

Mate 1: *"I feel like you do not care if I am too tired to have sex... you want it every night. I feel upset when you are not sensitive to how tired I am."*

Mate 2: *"I feel like you do not care that I am not getting enough sex. I know I want sex more than you do. I feel upset that you never seem to want it."*

- **Encourage exploration:**
  End by asking "What do you feel-think about this?"
    and start discussing it.

Mate 1: *"I do want to make love to you... just not when I am tired."*
Mate 2: *"I am frustrated because it seems like we rarely make love."*

2- **Agreement** is the goal of feedback is
    to move from words to actions.

- **Summarize the problem:**
  Each says what they think the problem
    is from their viewpoint.

Mate 1: *"I feel overwhelmed. I am always tired. When you want to make love at night... I have no energy left to do anything other than sleep."*

Mate 2: *"I feel frustrated. If we make love in the morning, I always have to look at the clock because I cannot afford to be late to work."*

- **Explore feelings:**
  Each shares their thoughts, feelings, and ideas
    about the problem.

Mate 1: *"I feel like we are not kids anymore. We cannot just take off and make love whenever you want to. We have responsibilities."*

Mate 2: *"I feel like we are not old folks either. If we wait until we are not tired, then we will never have any fun."*

- **Identify differences:**
  Both agree on where the points of disagreement are, what the problem is.

Mate 1: *"I feel - sometimes - like I am a prisoner of our routines. If we could get away and I could rest more... then we could enjoy making love."*

Mate 2: *"I feel better making love in our home... in our bed. It would be better if the kids could stay overnight at their grand-parents."*

- **Reach agreement:**
  Both agree that they genuinely want to work together to solve the problem.

Mate 1: *"I can ask my parents if they would take the kids this weekend. I could sleep in and then we could make love."*

Mate 2: *"I will look into places to get away to. Once we agree on where to go, I will ask my parents to take the kids for a weekend."*

3- **Action** is the result of feedback: to create actions that solve the problems.

- **State desired outcome:**
  Both state how they would like the
    problem to be solved.

Mate 1: "*I want to start our alone time at home. I would rest better if I was at home. I want to spend all day in bed and make love.*"

Mate 2: "*I want to get away to the hotel where we used to go before the kids were born. We could call for room service and stay in bed all day.*"

- **Pick from alternatives:**
  Both offer, discuss, and then pick from
    among alternative solutions.

Mate 1: "*I feel like we should arrange things as soon as possible. I will talk to my parents and see when they can take the kids.*"

Mate 2: "*I agree. I will get everything together so that, as soon as the kids are out of the house, we can get started on our party.*"

- **Determine evaluation:**
  Both agree on measures of success
    (how will we know that it works?)

The mates mark up a calendar for planned romantic getaways and list whether it will take place at home or out. Then they note if they were able to keep that date as well as how they would rate their getaway.

- **Schedule follow up:**
  Both set a time to see if their agreement is working or if it needs changing.

The mates agree to try their new system for a month and see how it works for them. They see what changes they can make to make the process better.

Example: Resolving WORK-LIFE Conflicts

Conflicts about work-life balance tend to come up daily. Each day each mate has to choose how much time and energy to devote to work (paid employment) and to life (outside of work). Each mate is bound to have different viewpoints on what is the best balance between work and life. These differences about the need to work and the desire to live are bound to create conflicts.

1- **Priorities:** You believe it is best to work when your employer calls (you live to work) or you believe it is best to have set hours (you work to live).

2- **Well Being:** You believe chores that contribute to your well-being are less important than work or you believe your well-being is more important than work.

3- **Chores:** You believe chores should be done by those best at doing them or you believe that chores should just be divided down the middle.

4- **Contribution:** You believe that whoever earns the most money contributes more or you believe that whoever is the most helpful contributes more.

If you and your mate have conflicts over work-life balance, look for differences in these areas. These are key to getting to the bottom of such issues.

1- **Accuracy** and honesty are the keys to this structured approach to feedback.

- **State the problem:**
  Start by using the "I" word as in "I feel..." or "I think..." or I believe..."

Mate 1: *"I feel like you love your work more than you love me."*
Mate 2: *"I feel like you love the kids more than you love me."*

- **Use specific details:**
  Continue by saying "I feel sad when you... said, did, forgot to do..."

Mate 1: *"I feel sad that you spend more time with your coworkers than you do with me or our children. I feel like we are never your priority."*

Mate 2: *"I feel angry that you are always hovering over the kids whenever we are together. I feel like I am never your priority."*

- **Encourage exploration:**
  End by asking "What do you feel-think about this?" and start discussing it.

Mate 1: *"I feel like our marriage is falling apart. Other people, even those at your work, spend more time with their families than you do."*

Mate 2: *"I feel like our marriage is falling apart. I feel like I am alone in our marriage... and I did not get married to feel lonely."*

2- **Agreement** is the goal of feedback is to move from words to actions.

- **Summarize the problem:**
  Each says what they think the problem is from their viewpoint.

Mate 1: *"I feel like you do not want to spend more time with us because you are so fascinated by your job... and it is all you care about."*

Mate 2: *"I feel like you do not want to spend more time with me because you are so possessive of our children... and they are all you care about."*

- **Explore feelings:**
  Each shares their thoughts, feelings, and ideas about the problem.

Mate 1: *"I wonder why you cannot find me and our kids as interesting as you find your job. When you are with us, you act like we are a chore."*

Mate 2: *"I wonder why you cannot find me as interesting as the kids. Remember when we used to talk about ideas: we never do that now."*

- **Identify differences:**
   Both agree on where the points of disagreement are, what the problem is.

Mate 1: *"It seems to me that you should spend more time with the family. That would mean you spending less time at work... each day."*

Mate 2: *"It seems to me that you should spend more time with me. That would mean you spending more time with me... romantically."*

- **Reach agreement:**
   Both agree that they genuinely want to work together to solve the problem.

Mate 1: *"I want to spend time with you: how can we do that?"*
Mate 2: *"I want to spend time with the family: how can we do that?"*

3- **Action** is the result of feedback: to create actions that solve the problems.

- **State desired outcome:**
  Both state how they would like the
     problem to be solved.

Mate 1: *"I want to spend more time with you:
     how about a date night?"*
Mate 2: *"I want to spend more time with the family:
     how about a family night?"*

- **Pick from alternatives:**
  Both offer, discuss, and then pick from
     among alternative solutions.

Mate 1: *"I want to spend more time with you:
     Saturday for date night?"*
Mate 2: *"I want to spend more time with the family:
     Friday for family night?"*

- **Determine evaluation:**
  Both agree on measures of success
     (how will we know that it works?)

The mates mark on a calendar each Saturday as to whether they had a date night and each mate rates it as to how fun it was for them. The whole family marks each Friday on a calendar as to whether they had a family night and all members of the family rate it as to how fun it was for them. Over time, the mates and the family can see what they enjoyed the most so they can repeat that activity.

- **Schedule follow up:**
  Both set a time to see if their agreement is working or if it needs changing.

The mates agree to try their new system for a month and see how it works for them. They see what changes they can make to make the process better.

Formula Part 2: About Active Listening

"The best way to understand people is to listen to them." (Ralph Nichols)

If you want to learn to really listen, start by actively listening to your mate: they just might surprise you. Better still, you will get to the bottom of the problem.

"Active Listening" is simple: just listen very closely to your mate. It goes beyond hearing the words that your partner speaks. It means showing them that you have understood and heard their meaning. Active Listening is a skill that is easy to learn... but it takes time and patience to put into practice.

<u>If you have tried the AAA method and are having trouble doing it, here is why:</u>

* **Mouth Shut, Mind and Ears Open:** One partner is not listening to their mate if - while their mate is speaking - they are always interrupting, criticizing, or composing their rebuttal. To listen actively, when your ears are open, your mouth should be shut and

your mind should be focused on your mate.

* **Understand What You Heard:** Show that you are listening by restating your partner's viewpoint back to them. Listen closely to see if they agree that what you heard is what they said. Unless you understand what your mate has said to you (and they agree you have): you have not really listened to them.

* **Clarify What You Heard:** Part of Active Listening is clarifying what you do not understand about what your partner has said to you. Ask questions and listen to answers. Do not stop until you and your mate are in agreement that you are "on the same page" and you are clearly understanding each other.

* **Reverse the Process:** If your partner wants you to actively listen to them... you should expect your partner to do the same Active Listening for you. Your mate will not really listen unless they can expect to be heard. Once you both get used to really listening to one another, you both will enjoy being truly heard (perhaps for the first time ever).

* **Focus:** When one mate is speaking, the other mate should focus on listening. The mate who is speaking should be the only one speaking until they finish. Then the roles should be reversed so that each is heard and understood.

EXAMPLE: If your mate complains that you do not listen to them, then do this Active Listening exercise.

One couple found that the best way for them to listen to each other was to turn off all distractions and talk/listen after their children were in bed. The person who was first to speak the last time was the first to listen the next time. This is the best chance for couples to do Active Listening.

1- Blocks to Active Listening

"Listen if you want to be heard." (John Wooden)

Active Listening is not as easy as it seems. There are many blocks to doing this process correctly. If one mate is convinced that another mate is not listening, then it is because the one not listening are engaging in the following behaviors:

* **Rehearsing:** As one mate speaks, the other mate is not listening if they are already preparing their response without listening to the entire speech.

* **Mind Reading:** As one mate speaks, the other mate is not listening if they keep on interrupting to anticipate their partner's point before it was made.

* **Filtering/Judging:** As one mate speaks, the other mate is not listening if they keep on dismissing each point that is made as it happens.

* **Advising/Sparring:** As one mate speaks, the other mate is not listening if they offer advice and/or objections as their partner speaks.

* **Placating/Negotiating:** As one mate speaks, the other mate is not listening if they are focus on calming their mate and/or bargaining for new terms.

* **"Defensive Listening":** If one mate is only listening for what they do not agree with, for inaccuracies, or for exaggerations, then they are not listening to their mate. They are engaged in one or more of the above blocks to listening.

EXAMPLE: When one mate is much older than their partner, the older mate will tend to exhibit these behaviors. The older mate can easily slip into the role of the parent, especially when it comes to judging, advising, and negotiating. If one mate acts like a parent - rather than a romantic partner - this will not only disrupt Active Listening, it will eventually erode the marital relationship.

2- Undermining Active Listening

"When people talk, listen completely. Most never listen." (Ernest Hemingway)
"There is a difference between listening and waiting for your turn to speak." (Simon Sinek)

Active Listening can be undermined by how the mate who listens is paying attention to the mate who speaks. If one mate is convinced that another mate is not listening, then it is because they are engaging in the following behaviors:

* **Facial Expressions:** While a smile is good, most other facial expressions (frowns, tears, rolling eyes, looks of shock, disgust, surprise, looking away, or lack of eye contact, etc) are dismissive. They will only convey your disinterest in what your mate has to say and it shows you are not listening to them.

* **Voice Inflections:** More than anything, a sarcastic, bitter, or judgmental tone of voice will powerfully convey your disinterest in what your mate has to say and shows you are not listening.

* **Body Positions:** Shrugging your shoulders, crossing arms or legs, turning your back, inattentive nodding, or constantly moving around are also dismissive and conveys disinterest.

* **Fidgeting/Mannerisms:** If you are looking at your phone, fiddling with papers, or tapping your fingers, this is dismissive and conveys disinterest.

* **Changing the Subject:** The mate who constantly changes the subject and refuses to stay on topic is not really listening to what their partner has to say.

* **Stonewalling/Daydreaming:** The mate who constantly avoids listening (stonewalling) or is inattentive (daydreaming) conveys disinterest.

EXAMPLE: One marriage ended very spectacularly when one mate admitted, during a session of Active Listening, that they did not want to be doing this activity. Their partner then said that they no longer wished to be married. Sadly, this couple started proceedings for divorce the very next day.

Formula Part 3: About Spoken Communication

"Communication is a skill that you can learn. If you're willing to work at it, you can rapidly improve your communication skill level. All it takes is time, practice, and patience!" (Brian Tracy)

Conversation with your mate can get stale over time. Here are some ways to get the conversational ball rolling between you. Most of your conversations should be pleasant ones... and here are proven ways to spark communication.

<u>If you have tried the AAA method and are having trouble doing it, here is why:</u>

* **Show Genuine Interest:** When you show by your questions and by your attitude that you are genuinely interested in getting to know your mate better, you are 90% on your way to improving the conversation with your mate.

> People just love to talk about themselves. When you are open to listening to what they have to say, conversation will flow easily between you.

* **Ask Good Questions:** Who? What? When? Where? Why? How? Questions that start with these

words elicit better answers than ones which require Yes, No, or Fine.

Asking questions which show you care about your mate and are sensitive to their concerns will create better conversations between you.

* **Match the Level:** When conversing with your mate, match the level of the intimacy in their speech. Some like to keep things light and on the surface, so do that. Others like to be serious and speak on meaningful topics, so you do the same.

Still others like to talk about their circle of friends, so join in. When you match the level of conversation of your mate, this increases their comfort level with you and it makes the conversation flow between you.

* **Be Positive:** Conversations drag when people talk about negative topics. For example, negative topics include "how all relationships suck", "how this couple's marriage is on the rocks", and so on. Good conversations should uplift and energize those involved in them, even when resolving conflict.

The only way this happens is to be positive. There must be an equal "give and take" between you and your mate because the essence of good conversation is the exchange of interesting ideas.

* **Give Genuine Compliments:** Praise is good only when it is sincere. If you are forcing yourself to compliment someone, they are sure to know it is false. To make compliments meaningful, praise a specific action. Say why you are praising them. For example, *"that was so nice of you to carry that lady's bag of groceries for her because she is not feeling well. You are the best!"*

EXAMPLE: <u>Here are some good conversation starters for married couples:</u>

- Ask: when do you need proof of my love the most and how can I show it?
- Tell your mate how they make you a better person and thank them.
- Ask: what do you enjoy doing with me? List the most enjoyable things first.
- Share a romantic fantasy with your mate and suggest trying it out.
- Ask: what have you always wanted to do and how can we make it happen?
- Tell your mate how much they have contributed to your life and how.
- Ask: what values are the most important to you in our life together?
- Share your ideal romantic date with your mate and go out on it.
- Ask: what is the one question you have always wanted the answer to?

Formula Part 4: About Effective Communication

"If you have nothing to say, say nothing." (Twain)
"If you have nothing good to say about someone else, then say nothing." (Anonymous)

<u>If you have tried the AAA method and are having trouble doing it, here is why:</u>

If you want your mate to hear you, here are more tips that will make your spoken communication so much more effective. These tips will help improve your communication with your mate... AND everyone else that you meet!

* **Be Polite:** Politeness puts others at their ease. When others feel as if you are treating them with kindness, they will automatically be more receptive to whatever you have to say... making your communication more effective.

* **Be Direct:** While still displaying good manners, when you can be short and to the point, you show others that you are respectful of their time. This keeps their interest level high... making your communication more effective.

* **Be Constructive:** To get what you want out of the communication, be sure to be constructive and positive. Enter the conversation by expecting that others want to help you and they will... making your communication more effective.

* **Be Honest:** Use the word "I" because this lets others know that this is your point of view. There is a huge difference between saying "You are ignoring me" (ineffective communication because it offends the other person) and "I feel like you are ignoring me" (effective communication from your viewpoint).

* **Be Clear:** You are clear when you use simple language, when you avoid jargon ("big, $10 words"), and when you use short sentences... so that a high school kid could understand you... making your communication more effective.

* **Be Comprehensive:** If communicating in person, use facial expressions and hand gestures to make your point. If communicating over the phone, use different inflections and pauses to make your speech interesting. If you are communicating in writing, use proper punctuation. If you are using a computer to write, use graphics because a "picture is worth 1,000 words." Being comprehensive makes your communication more effective.

* **Be Open:** To communicate, you have to really listen to others. Actively listening and being open to changing what you want to communicate based on the results of the conversation... makes your communication more effective.

* **Be Patient:** Repeating key points and slowing down or speeding up the pace as needed for your audience makes communication more effective.

* **Be Prepared:** The more you plan ahead by being ready for all potential scenarios and reactions from others, the more you will be able to direct the conversation to achieve your goals. The most effective communications are those which result in "win-win" results for the highest good of all.

EXAMPLE: There are many marriages where one mate believes that they are never at fault... and that their partner always is. Someone who is "always right" has little choice but to find fault with others.

In one couple, one mate blamed everyone and everything for their problems as follows. "You made me angry" (which is never true as anger is a choice made by an individual in response to a person or a situation). "This would not have happened if the kids [fill in the blank]" (children make mistakes and how an adult responds to it is their choice).

This marriage ended in divorce because the "always right" mate never took ownership or responsibility for how they contributed to the relationship issues.

Fight Fair: Resolving Conflicts Peacefully

"The person who has the most investment in the relationship (the most to lose if it ends) has the least control over it." (Counseling Mantra)

When it comes to "fighting", one partner always enters the arena with a natural advantage.

The one who has the least investment in the relationship has the upper hand when it comes to "winning" the conflict because they have the most control. Yet when one partner must win, the romantic relationship is always the loser.

For the relationship to win, both partners must follow this simple but time tested rule:
<u>"Complaining is good, criticizing is bad, resolving the conflict is the goal."</u>

Fighting Fair Part 1: Complaining is Good

"Discontent is the first step in the progress of a person or a nation." (Proverb)

The first part of "fighting fair" is "Complaining is good." Complaining means you are taking responsibility for your own feelings, behavior, and issues without blaming the other person. <u>Here is how to complain - FAIRLY!</u>

Use this formula, *"I feel _____, I think _____, and so I say/do _____ or fail to say/do _____ when you say/do _____ or fail to say/do _____."*

EXAMPLE: This is a good model for a complaint since it surfaces an issue without criticism. *"I feel sad when you leave the house without kissing me goodbye and so I say things I do not mean when you return home. I miss you kissing me and I hope you understand I need physical affection from you."*

Here is how you should complain to "fight fair" with your partner...

* **Take Ownership of Your Feelings:** Complaining in "fair fighting" means taking responsibility for your feelings. Since you are having the problem, keep focused on YOUR issue. Owning your feelings increases the intimacy between you and your partner. It keeps conflict from getting out of control.

* **Really Express Your Feelings:** Complaining in "fair fighting" means expressing what is going on inside you to the best of your ability. *Be honest:* tell your partner how you feel about what is going on. *Be clear:* explain your issues fully. *Be respectful:* help your partner understand your feelings and where you are coming from. Use EMOTION words: I feel [angry, hurt, sad, frustrated].

* **Listen Carefully to Your Partner:** Complaining in "fair fighting" means allowing your partner to express what is going on inside them. It really means NOT discounting their feelings by saying, *"You have no reason to feel that way..."* It means giving you both the space and time to express and resolve the feelings between you. Remember that FEELINGS do not have to be logical.

Here is how you should NOT complain because these complaints attack and belittle your partner...

* **Acting "Superior" to Your Partner:** Partners who are older than their mates, better educated, or are from "superior" backgrounds AND who claim these as reasons why their opinion should matter more... are fighting unfairly. A loving relationship only survives and thrives in an atmosphere of equality.

* **Questioning Your Partner's Competence-Motives:** Partners who attack their mate's character - accusing them of "bad motives", "hidden agendas", or "incompetence" - AND who use these reasons not to listen to what their mate has to say... are fighting unfairly. When you question your mate, you are saying that you cannot trust your mate and you do not have a real relationship.

* **Dredging Up Your Partner's History:** Partners who use their mate's past history - past failed relationships, past adulteries, or past addiction-illness - AND who claim these as reasons why their mates' opinion on a certain matter cannot be trusted or respected... are fighting unfairly. Mates should focus on the present. When the mates are not arguing about the present, they should talk through any unhealed past issues until they are resolved.

EXAMPLE: One way to deal with complaining is role reversal. One mate pretends to be their partner and imitates how their partner complains about them. Then the other mate does the same. Many times, each mate is quite surprised to hear how their partner imitates them as well as the content of the complaint (which they never heard before). It is a great way to open up a frank discussion that can resolve the complaints of both mates.

Fighting Fair Part 2: Criticizing is Bad

"Stop criticizing - it bores everybody else, does you no good, and doesn't solve problems." (Zig Ziglar)
"Just remember when you are criticizing or ignoring your mate, you are teaching them how to live without you." (Anonymous)

The second part of "fighting fair" is "Criticizing is bad." Criticizing is the opposite of complaining: destructive criticism means fixing blame and finding fault. It is attacking another for who they are and for what they hold dear.

The point of the attack is to divert attention from the attacker's shortcomings so that they will not have to change or compromise or deal with any complaints.

When you and your partner find yourselves descending into criticism, you need to say, *"We are discussing _____ and not _____."*

Keep coming back to the problem at hand... with the intention of solving it.

EXAMPLE: This is classic criticism. *"How can you know how hard it is for me at work? All you do is deal with kids all day and not real problems!"*

First, raising children means a mate is dealing with problems. Second, paid work outside the home is supported by unpaid work inside the home. Third, this kind of criticism does not and never will solve any problems because it avoids solving anything.

<u>Here is how you can avoid criticism and "fight fair" with your partner...</u>

* **Take Turns Talking:** Criticizing means failing to take turns talking. You should state your complaint in under two minutes. Any longer and you may shift from complaining into criticizing. If you and your mate are committed to solving problems as you go, then two minutes is enough to deal with new issues.

* **Give Equal Time:** "Fair fighting" should be like catch: one person talks while the other person just listens. Only one can hold the "conversational ball" at a time. This "ball" should not be held for any longer than two minutes at a time. When the time is up, the "ball" must be surrendered so that it always goes back and forth. <u>Take a tennis ball and pass it back and forth if you need to.</u>

* **Don't Play the "Blame Game":** When one partners uses blaming statements like "You always" or "You never" or "You should", that just shuts the other mate down. If you and your mate focus on fixing the blame, then you are not focused on fixing the problem and this will just keep the war going on between you. So, stop playing the blame game.

Here is how destructive criticism can seep into conflict resolution and how to stop it...

* **Mouth Shut While Mind and Ears are Open:** One mate is not really listening IF - while their mate is speaking - they are... constantly interrupting, composing their rebuttal, or cataloging their sins. To listen, when your ears are open, your mouth should be shut and your mind focused on the information.

* **Getting Off the Subject:** Focus on one issue at a time... that has arisen now-today. If you find yourself talking about what your partner did years ago, about how you still have not forgiven them, about how it is just the same argument, or about anything unrelated to the issue at hand, you are off the subject. Get back to the issue immediately.

* **Attacking Your Mate's Character:** If each are saying that the other is "too much of this" or "not enough of that" or "prone to do what's bad" or "prone to neglect to do what's good" and so on, you are attacking each other and cataloging sins. Stop it and get back to the issue at hand immediately.

SPECIAL NOTE: What is the difference between complaining and criticizing? Complaining is bringing up issues inside the relationship while criticizing is making personal attacks on and/or belittling a mate to avoid dealing with any complaints.

EXAMPLE: Those who attack with criticism almost never believe that they are doing it. If your partner is in denial about their habit of criticizing, shoot a video of them while they are doing it. When a person sees themselves on video, they usually see themselves differently. Often, this is enough for the mate who routinely criticizes, to reduce - or eliminate - their habit of destructive criticism.

1- Constructive Criticism (Counseling/Coaching)

"Every human being is entitled to courtesy and consideration. Constructive criticism is not only to be expected but sought." (Margaret Chase Smith)

Those who are the best in their field have learned to accept advice and constructive criticism (better known as counseling and/or coaching).

<u>Here is how to give and receive constructive criticism</u> (that which is meant for the highest good of you, your mate, and your relationship):

* **Accommodate:** Before the criticism even begins... the giver and receiver must prepare for it. The giver of the criticism should think long and hard about what they have to say... for every word of criticism will be hard on the receiver.

> The receiver of the criticism should be open to what they will hear... for when the criticism is constructive it is truly invaluable. Above all,

both the giver and receiver should expect that their communication will be positive and it will move their relationship to a better, stronger place going forward.

* **Agreement:** For criticism to be constructive... the giver and receiver must first agree on the issue at hand. The one who criticizes must clearly communicate what the issue is... so that the one who is criticized understands.

> Many times, when both parties try to agree on exactly what the issues are, they often end up resolving them. Remember where there is no mutual agreement on the issues, there can be no constructive criticism.

* **Appreciation:** Start out by being positive. Separate the good from the bad. Remember that the person who allows you to criticize them is opening their heart to you... and you should treat that with the utmost gentleness.

> **Begin** by praising the person for the good things they have done. **Continue** by being as positive as possible about the negative things you have to say. **End** by creating solutions that are win-win for both of you.

* **Acceptance:** The giver and the receiver of the criticism will know that it has succeeded when they both feel like the air has been cleared. The giver

will feel like they have been heard and understood. The receiver will feel like they have been respected and helped to move forward in a better way.

Both the giver and the receiver will have agreed to how things will be in the future to avoid the problems of the past. When they accept and act on their mutual solution, the criticism will have been proven to be constructive.

EXAMPLE: One couple, who both engaged in highly destructive criticism, decided to use the AAA technique and to commit to constructive criticism. By following the rules above, they stopped dreading their disagreements. Instead, they became more relaxed about their ability to discuss issues and this turned their relationship around. They told me later that this saved their marriage.

2- Destructive Criticism (Personal Attacks)

"The most destructive criticism is indifference." (E. W. Howe)

Destructive criticisms live far after the words are spoken. Here is how to know when criticism is destructive (when it is only intended to hurt):

* **Aggressiveness, Not Assertiveness:** Those who deliver constructive criticism do so from the standpoint of assertiveness (standing up for their personal rights and beliefs).

Those who deliver destructive criticism do so from the standpoint of aggressiveness. They use it to control others (by bullying them), to gain their approval (through instilling fear), or to feel secure (by making others feel like they are "less" so that they can be "more").

* **Adversary, Not Ally:** Those who deliver constructive criticism act like an ally: they are kind, friendly, and act with your best interests at heart.

Those who deliver destructive criticism are your adversaries. They want to tear you down, break your spirit, and promote their own selfish agenda at your expense. They will use shame, guilt, fear, and anger to control you. They do not have your best interests at heart: that they are using destructive criticism against you is proof positive of this. You are wise to never let anyone influence you who does not like you.

* **Anger, Not Advice:** Those who deliver constructive criticism are trying to give you advice that will help you make your life better.

Those who deliver destructive criticism are trying to feel better themselves by venting their anger, hurt, fear, and frustration on others. You are wise to realize that others who criticize in a destructive manner are just trying to pass on their pain to anyone else who is around them.

* **Argument, Not Agreement:** Those who deliver constructive criticism are trying to end arguments by creating agreements that will improve the relationship in the future. They want a mutually satisfying solution.

> Those who deliver destructive criticism do not want to create agreements, they want to continue arguing. Maybe they prefer living on the choppy seas of their emotions. Maybe they believe arguments are a way of showing love. Maybe they argue because it makes them feel connected and engaged. You are wise to remember: nothing justifies destructive criticism.

EXAMPLE: Mates who talk - even if it is in anger - deep down - want to save their relationship. Yet, destructive criticism - that is not stopped - will end a relationship eventually. Before the relationship ends in divorce, the mates will just stop talking once it has become too late to save their marriage.

Fighting Fair Part 3: Resolving Conflict

"Where conflicts are identified, they will be resolved." (Betsy DeVos)

The most important part of this rule is that "Resolving the conflict is the goal."

Here is how to work toward resolving conflicts:

* **Agree to Fight Fairly:** Resolving conflict means being willing to admit when you are not fighting fairly. If you can only complain by belittling your mate, if you can only criticize by cataloging your mate's sins, and if you can only argue in ways that keep the conflict alive between you... then you are not fighting fairly. You need to stop doing all that.

* **Stay On Track:** If you or your mate find you are fighting unfairly, stop it! If one mate calls their partner out for fighting unfairly, it must be done with loving kindness. The "offending" partner should stop it and both should commit to getting back on track! BOTH partners need to work together.

* **Become Part of the Solution:** Resolving conflict means compromising and working toward solutions. Stop trying to win and start focusing on what is really important: your relationship. Tell your partner what you will do/give up that they want if they do/give up something you want. Keep going until you have resolved the issue(s) between you in a way that each partner gets some of what they want.

* **Focus on the Outcome:** Whatever happens, both partners must keep coming back to the goal: <u>a mutually agreeable solution to the problem</u>. This can only be achieved by getting to the root of the issue, by using positive communication, and by negotiating a consensus that "everyone can live with."

* **Do Not Withdraw:** Men will tend to withdraw from resolving conflicts if they feel threatened: they will just end the argument and walk away. Women will tend to withdraw if they feel hopeless: they will just become compliant and "go along to get along." Withdrawal leads to the end of the relationship.

EXAMPLE: As long as a couple is talking with one another, even negatively, they are still participating in the relationship. Negative communication between mates is an attempt - by both of them - to pull one another into their reality and get the relationship to be what they want it to be. The relationship is over when on mate is done with communicating: they do not wish to hear what their partner has to say and they do not wish to respond to issues. The mate who does not speak is saying that the relationship is over... once and for all.

Fighting Fair Part 4: Dealing with Difficulties

"Much unhappiness has come into the world because of things left unsaid." (Fyodor Dostoyevsky)
"The bitterest tears shed over graves are for words left unsaid and deeds left undone." (Harriet Beecher Stowe)

You cannot get what you do not ask for. You cannot get what you ask for unless you believe you will. Honest communication is never wasted. Communication is not always easy.

Here is how to deal with difficulties in fighting fair.

* **About Saying No:** If you say "No" and get your mate to understand what is in your mind and heart (why you said "No"), this can strengthen your relationship. If you offer your mate suggestions about where else to go -or- what else to do to get what they want, your mate most likely will not hold that "No" against you.

* **Being Forthright:** If you answer your mate instead of avoiding them, they are more rather than less likely to trust you. They will come to respect you. Often, if you can express yourself with kindness and gentleness, your mate may take your unpleasant news without bursting into anger or without ignoring you.

* **Compassion Counts:** If you appeal to the understanding, the charity, and the compassion of your mate, they will surprise you by being more understanding, loving, and forgiving than you would expect. When you expect your mate will hear you with an open mind and heart, they are more likely to.

* **Dealing with Doubt:** If you share your thoughts with your mate, they are more apt to sympathize with you than criticize you. Sharing yourself more with others (especially with your mate) can only continue to improve your relationships. Expect they will listen to you instead of doubting if they can.

* **Expectations:** If you believe you will not get what you are asking for, that sets up negative energy which contributes to the unwanted result. Many times others will mirror your own energy back to you just as they will return your positive energy. Expect your mate will hear/listen to you… and it will be so.

* **Focus:** Remember that you always get from life what you focus on with your thoughts, feelings, and actions. Unless you communicate with a positive focus, you cannot get what you want. If you believe that your mate will not listen to you or give you want you want, then it is time to rethink your relationship.

EXAMPLE: In general, women tend to have difficulty in saying "No" while men have difficulty in sharing their true thoughts. These behaviors are often socially or culturally driven. "Mothers" are supposed to care for others more than they do for themselves. "Fathers" are supposed to "know best" and to never show doubt or weakness. Yet, these kinds of stereotypes often lead to unhappiness because they burden people with enormous stress. If you find yourself being stressed by these roles: choose to act differently and see what happens.

Making Decisions Together:
Rules to Resolve Conflicts Peacefully

Decisions Part 1: Reaching Consensus

"Not cohabitation but consensus constitutes marriage." (Cicero)

Consensus is defined as "a decision making process that works creatively to include all persons in reaching the solution because all persons must agree to the final decision." Below are the key features of the consensus building process that mates can use to make important decisions.

* **Shared Participation:** Consensus "promotes participation between partners because each one has the power to make changes in the relationship and/or to prevent changes that they find to be unacceptable." Instead of one partner always calling all the shots, in consensus, both partners must genuinely agree.

* **Resolution of Relationship Issues:** Consensus "gives each partner the chance to listen, to be heard, and to address one another's concerns instead of moving past them." Since both partners' concerns are important, consensus leads to solutions that are acceptable to both partners.

* **The Show Stopper:** What makes Consensus work is that "a single 'Major Objection' stops a suggested course of action from being taken." A "Major Objection" means one partner "cannot live with the suggested course of action" and so the mates must find other alternatives (beside the major objection) that are acceptable to both.

* **No Winners, No Losers:** The idea of "win-lose" only keeps conflict alive. In win-lose, the winning partner wins by "steam-rolling" over the loser creating resentment in the loser and the desire to win the next time. In consensus, there are no winners and no losers... except for the relationship which is the winner.

* **Essence of Consensus:** Ideals of consensus are "empowering versus overpowering", showing "loving versus exercising power", and reaching "mutual agreement versus individual victory or defeat." If you both love one another other, then each of you should want to be happy in the relationship.

EXAMPLE: A consensus driven solution is one that neither mate really likes but one that both can live with... to preserve the relationship.

For example, people show love to their mates in different ways. Some mates like to hear the words "I love you" while others like to get gifts from their mate or do tasks for them.

For example, one couple the husband gave his wife gifts... but he would not say words of love while the wife said words of love but did not give him many gifts. They reached a consensus whereby they would reverse roles from time to time with the husband speaking words of love and the wife giving gifts. This decision made them both happy.

Decisions Part 2: Creating Compromise

"All compromise is based on give and take, but there can be no give and take on fundamentals. Any compromise on true fundamentals is a surrender. For it is all give and no take." (Gandhi)

Compromise is what makes consensus driven solutions work.

Here is what makes compromise work...

* **Giving versus Giving-In:** "Giving" is compromise: you give something and your mate gives something so that you both get something. "Giving" makes compromise work and creates lasting relationships.

> "Giving-in" is not compromise: if you must give and not get, you are giving-in while if your mate must give and not get, they are giving-in. "Giving-in" undermines compromise and damages and/or breaks apart relationships.

* **Assertiveness versus Aggressiveness:** "Assertiveness" is compromise: you state your point of view with the complete confidence that your mate will understand and consider your viewpoint and that they will do the same for you.

> "Aggressiveness" is not compromise: it happens when you or your mate pummels each other in accepting an unchanging point of view.

"Aggressiveness" undermines compromise and damages and/or breaks apart relationships.

* **Acceptance versus Begrudging:** "Acceptance" is compromise: once the compromise is reached, you and your mate accept and implement it.

"Begrudging" is not compromise: if one or both still wants to argue then a solution has not been reached. "Begrudging" kills compromise and keeps arguments alive which will damage and/or break apart relationships.

EXAMPLE: If you are fighting about something, make sure it is something worth risking your relationship over. I have seen loving relationships break up over the most trivial of items.

For example, a husband gave his wife a blue fan as an anniversary gift. Their daughter wanted to wear the blue fan as an accessory to her wedding dress because it was "old and blue" and as the wife contended "borrowed." When their daughter returned from her honeymoon, she refused to return the fan, claiming that it was had been a wedding gift.

This unleashed a series of nasty fights that spread throughout the entire family over a blue fan. In the end, the husband bought his wife another fan and this compromise ended the family conflict. Yet, this almost broke the family apart.

Decisions Part 3: Building Cooperation

"When love and skill work together, expect a masterpiece." (John Ruskin)

What makes mates true partners is working together like a team. When mates are cooperating, together everyone achieves more.

Cooperation is not something that comes naturally, the team must work toward it.

* **Thinking as We Instead of I:** To establish a partnership with your mate, both of you must shift from thinking in terms of what "I" want to do to thinking in terms of what "we" want to do. That means decisions must be made more slowly to give mates time to discuss and agree on what to do.

* **What is Best for Us:** Becoming "we" means doing what is best for BOTH as a couple. Sometimes this means each will end up doing things they would not do on their own... and may not like very much. Yet you both do those things because you are acting as a couple and you are doing what is "best for us."

* **Achieving Our Goals:** Cooperation comes from both mates being focused on achieving "our" goals as a couple. When both partners row their boat of life together in the same direction, miracles result.

EXAMPLE: Be honest with yourself and answer this question. "Do you want to do what YOU want to do -or- do you want to do what WE want to do?"

If your relationship is important to you, then you want to do what WE want to do. In other words, you must freely choose to cooperate with your mate... or your relationship will not work. For a relationship to succeed, over time, it must balance out to 50% of what you want to do and 50% of what your mate wants to do. If you are not comfortable with that, then you are better off on your own.

Giving/Receiving Forgiveness:
Rules to Resolve Conflicts Peacefully

Forgiveness Part 1: Charity Begins at Home

"He that cannot forgive others breaks the bridge over which he must pass himself; for every man has need to be forgiven." (Thomas Fuller)

* **Look in Mirror:** Others are only mirrors for the relationship that we have with ourself. Part of why we are drawn so irresistibly to our mates is that we see ourselves most clearly reflected in their mirror.

What they show us is why we should love ourselves and how we have failed to do so. Mates can help us to love and forgive ourselves. Yet this charity (self love) must begin at home before it can reach out to others, especially to a mate.

Here is what we will see in our mate's mirror... and what can be done to increase our own self love and, as a result, improve our communication.

* **Heal the Past:** Like and believe it or not, critical events in your past will cast their shadow on the way you relate to others in the present. Others, especially mates, will trigger those open unhealed wounds from the past.

> If you and your mate choose to confront and heal these issues together, you will build up your intimacy and closeness. If not, your unhealed wounds will continue to cause you both unnecessary suffering until you heal them.

* **Forgive the Present:** The answer to all our relationship problems lies deep down inside ourselves. We tend to blame our mate for things that we have not forgiven in ourselves.

> Lack of self forgiveness and self love is the root cause of misunderstandings and needless conflicts between loving mates. Forgiving yourself first is the only way that you will be able to forgive anyone else, your mate included.

* **Empower the Future:** Charity to yourself always leads to greater self awareness and increased self love. This empowers your future by enabling you to give more love to all significant others in your life.

When you overreact to "perceived failings" in others, you have found new areas inside yourself that must be healed. The more you heal yourself, the more life will "turn around" bringing you to your greatest joy.

EXAMPLE: Many marriages break up because one partner has been so severely abused - physically, mentally, emotionally - that they cannot get past it. Such damaged people are not able to give or receive love, not even to a mate that they deeply and genuinely care for... and do not want to lose.

If you or your mate have suffered abuse of any kind and you both want to save your marriage, then you are well advised to go for individual counseling to resolve the wounds from your past.

Forgiveness Part 2: Stop Keeping Score

"Keeping score is for games, not friendships." (John C. Maxwell)

Keeping score is for sporting events not for loving relationships. Keeping score prevents you from giving and receiving the forgiveness that is so necessary to lasting, happy relationships.

<u>Here is why keeping score of "who was right and who was wrong" in a relationship just shuts down communication:</u>

* **Nobody Wins:** Unlike in a game, when people keep score in a relationship, nobody wins. Often what happens is that everyone loses. The one who keeps score nurses past grudges instead of forgiving them. The one scored with making errors feels like there is no hope of ever redeeming their past mistakes or of doing right in the future.

* **Mired in Unforgiveness:** Keeping score short circuits forgiveness - which is a positive, present-oriented state of existence - and keeps people mired in unforgiveness - which is a negative, past-centered state of existence. Keeping score ensures that both partners stay mired in reliving a fixed past event that can never be changed. It will totally block communication in the end.

* **Focusing on the Score Card:** Perhaps the worst thing that scoring does is to put partners on the defensive. They are so fearful of what is going to end up on their score card that they spend too much time in justifying what they did/did not do and in planning what they will do to even the score and keep the fight going. Score keeping ends up destroying even the most loving relationships.

EXAMPLE: When he was a young boy, a husband got into the habit of writing down every incident of his abuse and/or neglect from his parents. This saved his life because he was removed from his home and placed in foster care with better people.

Yet he never stopped writing about those around him. When he got married, he started writing about his wife. At first, understanding why he did it, his wife accepted it. After a while, she became tired of her husband reading from his book about her whenever they fought. So, she gave him a choice: give up his book... or give up their marriage. They ended up burning his book.

Forgiveness Part 3: Cultivating Calmness

"The more tranquil a man becomes, the greater is his success, his influence, his power for good." (James Allen)

Never communicate while you are angry because you are CERTAIN to say things that you do not mean and cannot take back. Before you speak, try cultivating calmness first. This alone is bound to improve your relationship communication because it will shift you out of anger and into calmness.

* **Sight Oriented People** (NLP Visual Recallers) should use...

* **Breaths:** The quickest way to relax is by taking deep breaths which will bring more life into your body. This will balance your heart rate, hormones, blood pressure, and adrenaline which are elevated by anger. This will calm you down and help you to think more clearly before you speak with your mate.

* **Guided Imagery:** Visualize an experience you know will be profoundly relaxing for you. Whether it comes from your memory or your imagination, the key is to fill your awareness - using as many senses as possible (see it, hear it, touch it, etc) - with whatever is guaranteed to make you deeply happy. Connecting with joy will calm you down.

* **Hearing Oriented People** (NLP Auditory Recallers) should use...

* **Self Talk:** You can cultivate calmness by "talking yourself into it." That is done by saying to yourself silently or out loud "Relax", "Calm Down", "Take it Easy", and so on. Put your fingers to your heart and feel your heart slow down its pounding. This will help you to cultivate the relaxation response.

* **Music:** Listen to calming relaxing music. The key is to listen to the "right" music which will put you into states of greater harmony. Not all music has this capability... there is special relaxation music (which attunes you to the earth) and the best of it is created by composer Steven Halpern.

* **Touch Oriented People** (NLP Kinesthetic Recallers) should use...

* **Stress "Toys":** For those who like to be hands on, stress toys are a great way to calm down. These include: "worry stones" which can be rubbed, hand vices which can be pressed, rubber balls which can

be squeezed, and so on. It is better to take out your anger on a stress toy than on your mate.

* **Exercise:** If the situation allows it, focus your awareness on relaxing your muscles. There are many meditative practices (like yoga) you can do to calm your mind by relaxing your muscles. If you practice these exercises, you can use them to calm your anger before you speak with your mate.

EXAMPLE: Do the "Hong Sah" Breath for Calming:

1- Inhale through the nose to the count of ten.
2- While inhaling, mentally repeating the word, "Hong" as you inhale.
3- Hold the breath to the count of 10.
4- Exhale slowly through the mouth as you repeat the word, "Sah" out loud.

Forgiveness Part 4: About Confession

"Confession of errors is like a broom which sweeps away the dirt and leaves the surface brighter. I feel stronger for having confessed." (Gandhi)

Secrets are like weights on the heart, especially inside romantic relationships. These weights only can be lifted by honest and sincere confessions.

"A little confession is good"... for the romantic relationship. No matter how hard someone tries - from time to time - everyone ends up saying or

doing things they should not do -or- failing to say or do things they should do.

Acknowledging where our actions fell short of our intentions - and sincerely wanting to do better the next time - builds intimacy and trust between mates.

These turn confessions into relationship healers:

* **Coming Clean:** Confession is the recognition of a problem and the willingness to take ownership of it. Coming clean is being honest about what you have said or done -or- what you failed to say or do that ended up hurting your partner. Coming clean is revealing the reasons that motivated your actions or inactions and expecting your partner to understand.

* **Expecting Kindness:** If you confessing to a personal fault, expect that your partner will treat your confession with an open heart. If you are hearing a confession, listen to it with an open mind. In the future, roles will be reversed... and so what you sow this time, you will reap the next time.

* **Making It Better Next Time:** Saying that things will be better next time means nothing unless it is also backed up by a plan of action. Looking at what went wrong, finding what caused the problem, and deciding what can be done to "make it better next time" is what makes the confession truly sincere.

* **Sin No More:** If you and/or your mate keeps on repeating the same mistakes, confessing them loses impact. To make a confession sincere, words must be followed by actions that support them.

> In the long run, insincere "lip service" will poison and eventually kill a relationship. It is best to go away and "sin no more" after you have confessed. Regular, sincere confession can keep the lines of communication between partners open, flowing, and growing.

EXAMPLE: Here is an example of one mate confessing to their partner about having had an extra-marital affair. When it comes to infidelity, these are five questions that the "cheating mate" needs to answer as honestly as possible:

1- *"Have you ended the affair?"* The answer must be "yes" or do not confess. You cannot have a solid marriage while you cheat on your mate.

2- *"WHY did you feel the need to have the affair?"* Most affairs happen because the "cheating mate" is not getting something "they need" from their partner. If there is something wrong inside the marriage, the "cheating mate" needs to be clear about what that is. The mate who was "cheated on" must decide if they can or even want to "fix" the problem so that the marriage can move forward.

3- _"Do you regret your behavior and sincerely want to make amends?"_ The answer must be "yes" and specific actions to make amends must be stated.

4- _"Are you willing to do whatever it takes to earn your partner's trust back and rebuild your relationship?"_ The answer must be "yes" and specific actions to repair the relationship must be stated and agreed upon.

5- _"Are you ready to commit yourself to your relationship and be faithful?"_ The answer must be "yes" or accept the end of your relationship.

Tools for Loving Communication

Being a Relationship Hero

"Lord, make me an instrument of your peace. Where there is hatred, let me sow love; Where there is injury, pardon." (Francis of Assisi)

Before you learn the tools for loving communication, there is one important question you must ask yourself. Are you ready to be a relationship hero?

* **What is Your Priority?:** At some point in their relationship, each partner must make the choice of whether they would rather be right (sticking to their own viewpoint) or be in relationship (by forgiving the past, by being willing to change for the relationship, and by creating a mutually acceptable resolution).

* **Let Peace Begin with Me:** Never go to bed on your anger. When you make a habit of resolving the differences between you each day, this stops resentments from building up inside the relationship. The "hero" is the partner who is the first one to declare peace when there is a dispute between the mates. The "hero" is the one who values creating peace - by coming up with solutions - rather than prolonging the war inside the relationship.

* **Let Understanding Begin with Me:** Try hard to see things from your partner's point of view. No matter how close two people are, they are bound to see things differently and this creates conflict. The "hero" is the partner who is the first one to connect with the other mates' point of view and understand why they think-feel the way they do. The "hero" is the one who uses that understanding to compromise and to get the relationship back on track.

* **Let Forgiveness Begin with Me:** Forgiveness flows from understanding. Forgiveness is not forgetting what happened. Forgiveness is not condoning what happened. Forgiveness is letting go of any anger and disharmony out of love for the other person. The "hero" forgives and starts over by doing different things and by doing things differently. In this way, the relationship can be purged of anger and can - once again - be grounded in love.

* **Let Healing Begin with Me:** Healing means "where there is hatred, let me sow love…" The

"hero" is the partner who is the first one to bring more love into the situation by choosing to be an instrument of peace. "What can I do to make things better between us?" is the question the "hero" asks.

"How can we bring more peace and love into our relationship?" is the next question the "hero" asks. The honest answers to these questions is where the healing process truly begins.

EXAMPLE: When your communication with your mate is not what it should be and you both want to improve your relationship, then you need to start by not going to bed on your anger.

Take 30 minutes before you go to sleep to discuss whatever issues are between you and resolve your anger as much as you can. Once you start reducing the issues between you, the time you need for such discussions will decrease. So, is your relationship worth 30 minutes a day?

Tools Part 1: Compliments

There is a time for resolving problems and issues... and there is a time for remembering why you fell in love in the first place.

<u>Here are the time honored ways for mates to build up the romantic communication between them:</u>

1- Importance of Compliments

"There is more hunger for love and appreciation in this world than for bread." (Mother Teresa)

With each word that is spoken between mates, they either move towards each other or away from each other in their relationship. When you have arguments, you are exchanging negative words that move you away from one another.

Compliments are a way of exchanging positive words that move you toward one another. They will help to undo the damage of any negative speaking.

You will have noticed that compliments have already been mentioned. This is because compliments are one of the greatest (and easiest) tools for improving communication of any kind, especially with a mate.

<u>Here is what happens when you give a compliment to your mate:</u>

1- **Compliments Powerfully Communicate Love:** When compliments are sincere, they move mates closer together and strengthen their bond to one another. Every mate likes to hear that their hard work for the family is noticed and appreciated. Every mate wants to see that they are appreciated for their unique qualities like their kindness, their wisdom, and their skills.

Ask yourself: are you and your mate arguing with each other more than you are appreciating each other with compliments? If true, then you need to argue less and compliment each other more to build up your relationship.

2- Compliments Create a Positive Environment: Compliments generate a positive space around the couple. The more sincere compliments there are, the more positive the space becomes. When the space is positive, negative arguments are more noticeable and become more painful to engage in.

Ask yourself would you rather live in a positive space or exist in a negative one? The choice is yours: you both make it one word at a time.

3- Compliments are Motivational: When someone is complimented, it makes them desire another compliment... and motivates them to do something to get another one. It helps each mate to do something much better than before. For example, if you praise your mate's cooking, they will want to make more of the complimented food for you.

Ask yourself: what does it cost you to give a sincere compliment? Giving a compliment is free... and it is also priceless.

4- Compliments Do Good/Feel Good: Want to raise your mood? Compliment someone (especially yourself). When you do good, it feels good... not only for you but for the person receiving your compliment (even if you are the one complimented).

> Ask yourself: when you see something to compliment in someone else, does it raise their self esteem and boost yours? It does. You could not have seen the good in someone else unless you saw it in yourself first. As your view of others becomes more positive you will feel more positive too.

EXAMPLE: One client once told me "I never get compliments. I think if I do enough good, people will notice it, and just compliment me." I replied with a compliment to her and said, "Try giving out some compliments and see what happens." Sure enough the compliments she gave out came back to her.

2- How to Give Compliments

"People don't usually compliment your character: they should." (Anonymous)

If you want to give your mate a genuine compliment, here is what keep in mind.

1- **Make an "I" Compliment to "You":** If you say, "you did [whatever it is to be praised]," you are making a "you" statement. This can come across like judging rather than complimenting. It's better to begin with "I" as follows:

"I appreciate you for
  [doing something awesome]
  [what - when - how you did it]."
"I like how [you did something helpful]
  [what - when - how you did it]."
"I am grateful to you because
  [you did something helpful]
  [what - when - how you did it]."
"I feel you were so kind when
  [you did something helpful]
  [what - when - how you did it]."
"I am proud of you because
  [you did something great]
  by [what - when - how you did it]."
"I am inspired by you because
  [you did something great]
  by [what - when - how you did it]."
"I like your [choice or action in the situation]
  because [reason why]."
"Thank you for [doing something great]
  [what - when - how you did it]."

2- **Be Genuine:** People can tell right away when you do not mean what you say. <u>So say what you mean and mean what you say.</u> People will believe your compliment when they can feel that it comes from your heart.

3- **Be Specific:** Being specific in your compliment helps it sound more genuine. It shows the person that you are paying close attention to what they did or did not do. When you praise a person for a specific thing (like helping them when it was needed), they are more likely to do that specific activity again for you. Compliments are motivational!

4- Be Timely: Compliments are more powerful when they are given immediately because the link between the act and the compliment is clear. Try to do it in front of others because this kind of "social proof" validates the compliment even further.

5- Be Consistent: Deliver the compliment with a smile and a warm voice. Be sure to make friendly eye contact. If appropriate, give them a gentle reassuring (non-sexual) touch.

6- Be Respectful: Focus on the person respectfully by complimenting such things as their character traits, their accomplishments, and their positive effect on you and others (not trivial things like clothes or makeup). Do not make the compliment at all about you (this looks like you are just fishing for compliments and it devalues the compliment itself).

7- Avoid Backhanded Compliments: Make sure your compliment is not at all offensive (example. "You look nice for someone so old..." or "you look better that ugly dress"). If you cannot give a kind or positive compliment, then it is best to say nothing.

EXAMPLE: Here are some compliments that are sure to please your mate:

"I am constantly thinking about you."
"I am grateful you are always inside my heart."
"I am so lucky to have you in my life."
"I know that you are the perfect one for me."
"No one makes me happier than you do."
"Know that your love is everything to me."
"My love, you take my breath away."
"When I am with you, nothing else matters."
"I want to spend the rest of forever with you."
"When we hug, I wish we never had to let go."

3- Problems with Compliments

"Compliments are one measure of an individual's ability to give and receive love. If you cannot give or receive a compliment, you are in trouble." (Proverb)

* **Low on Love:** Those who never give compliments usually cannot give what they have never received. They are "too low on love" because they have received little or none from their family/caregivers.

> So they have no love to give out because they need to keep what precious little love they have inside... for themselves. The truth is you cannot give what you do not have.

* **Internal Conflict:** Those who cannot receive any compliments feel badly about themselves. If a person believes inside that they are truly worthless, they will feel intensely uncomfortable when they hear praise about how worthwhile they are.

This internal conflict will make them resist giving or receiving compliments. In fact, they may distrust whoever compliments them.

* **False Obligations:** Those who cannot give compliments to others are concerned that such praise will create an obligation.

> They think *"if I say something nice to [person], then that individual will expect that I will have to [give them money or property, do unpleasant tasks for them, or, in the end, somehow be taken advantage of]."* So rather than give a compliment, they stay silent.

* **Ethical Training:** Those who cannot receive compliments from others have been taught by their religion, culture, or community that it is wrong to receive praise because it leads to the sin of pride.

> So rather than go against their personal ethics, these individuals will go out of their way to avoid any kind of compliment. In fact, they will avoid people who do give out compliments.

* **Fulsome Praise:** Those who cannot give compliments to others are concerned that praise will make them sound fake, phony, or dishonest. They believe that giving praise will make them seem like a "suck up" who is only trying to give kind words only to get something in return (like a false obligation).

* **Gender Bias:** "Real" men are not supposed to want praise for doing "what a man should do": he should just do it and take pride in his manliness. "Real" women are just supposed to support others because they "Mrs" Some Man or Some Kid's Mom: she should just take pride being a good wife-mother-daughter-sister (another block to compliments).

The bottom line is that if you and/or your mate cannot give and receive compliments then you should seek counseling help immediately.

EXAMPLE: I have seen marriages break up over one mate's inability to accept and appreciate compliments from the other. The mate who always gives the compliment ends up feeling that the mate who does not (or cannot) accept or acknowledge their compliment really does not love them... and so it erodes their relationship.

Tools Part 2: Courtesy

"A man is known by his deeds. A good deed is never lost; he who sows courtesy reaps friendship, and he who plants kindness gathers love." (Basil)

Each person is an opportunity for you to practice kindness and courtesy, especially your mate.

Here are some easy ways to do this:

1- Courtesy in Words

"The small courtesies sweeten life; the greater ones ennoble it." (Christian Nestell Bovee)

* **Warm Greetings:** When mates part for the day, they should kiss and hug goodbye and then kiss and hug hello. This show mates they are each other's top priority. Each kiss and each hug moves the couple closer together.

* **Kind Words:** What kind word you can say to your mate? Say things like "Please", "Thank you", "I appreciate your help", "I am grateful to you", "You are so awesome", and so on. Say them like you mean them (because you should!).

* **Love Notes:** Write a short message (see text messages below) on a note and hide it somewhere that your mate is sure to find it (ex. in a wallet or purse). This little gesture can reap big dividends in the happiness of your relationship.

* **Love Notes:** Send a text message to your mate when they are sure to be checking their phone. The nice thing about text messages is that you can add colorful emojis to them which will spice up the message to your mate.

* **Good Manners:** Act as if you were a role model of proper conduct. Be on time. Be prepared. Be courteous. Be respectful. Be fully present wherever you are. Be thankful for the gift of your mate!

* **Good Opportunities:** Create "win-win" scenarios wherever you go. Be willing to forgive wrongs done to you by anyone, especially your mate. Be grateful for praise and blessings. Be generous where you can. Share what you know to smooth your mate's path and make their life more harmonious.

* **Genuine Compliments:** Give compliments generously. Everyone does something well. Everyone has a special quality or talent. Everyone can use praise... and rarely do they get enough! <u>The need to give genuine compliments to your mate cannot be stressed enough!</u>

EXAMPLE: Here is a creative way to send a love note. Use the first letter of your mate's name to write loving things to them. Here is an example:

K... For the many **K**indnesses she shows me...
    as unworthy as I am to be receiving them.
A... For **A**lways standing by me...
    especially when other have abandoned me.
T... For speaking the **T**ruth to me always...
    even when I do not wish to hear it from her.
E... For the **E**normous burdens she helps me carry...
    I could not live a single moment without her.

2- Courtesy in Actions

"Courtesies of a small and trivial character are the ones which strike deepest in the grateful and appreciating heart." (Henry Clay)

* **Kind Actions:** What act of kindness can you do for your mate? Ask them how you can help them to make their life easier. Do a favor for your mate in taking on a task that you know they do not like to do. Help them with their chores.

* **Thoughtful Actions:** Give to your mate what you would like to receive in their place. Make it a point to cheer them up. Remember their birthdays and their other key anniversaries. Help them to feel special and important.

* **Flowers or Candy:** Take a moment to put a flower or a piece of candy where your mate is sure to find it and/or arrange to have it delivered. Everyone always appreciates any gifts of thoughtfulness that are sent just brighten up their day.

* **Taking Classes:** Where you and your mate share interests, taking a class together to learn more about it. Couples who working on communication can benefit from taking a class on meditation so that they can learn how to calm down before they discuss their relationship issues. Working on a shared class together is bonding.

* **Date Nights:** If you are not getting out of the house to spend time with your mate, then you need to. It does not have to involve spending lots of money. It does involve you and your mate spending concentrated time together doing what you enjoy.

* **Joint Showers:** If your shower is large enough, showering together where each of you cleans the other off (no monkey business), creates closeness.

* **Loving Touch:** Giving your mate a quick massage on their temples, hands, feet, or back and receiving the same in return from your mate quickly shows love. Five minutes of loving touch is enough to energize mates.

EXAMPLE: "Monarch for the Day" is an act of service where one mate who is the monarch gets served by their partner all day. Whatever the monarch says goes (at least for what can be reasonably be performed by their mate in a single day). It is the ultimate in pampering your mate and is fun for you as well (monarchs are notorious in requiring sexual favors of their obedient servants). Of course, mates will later switch roles (the former monarch will then become the servant).

Tools Part 3: Compassion

1- About Compassion to Your Mate

"If you want others to be happy, practice compassion. If you want to be happy, practice compassion." (Dalai Lama)

"The desire to help another out of love and love alone" is the best description of what it means to have and show compassion. If there is one single

trait that defines a loving relationship, it is the mates' deep compassion for one another.

There are many ways to show compassion.

<u>Here are some of the best:</u>

* Instead of saying "I love you" to your mate, ask:
    "How can I help you?
      How can I make things better?"

* Instead of defending your position to your mate,
    consider surrendering your position to theirs...
    for love's sake.

* Instead of choosing to be right,
    choose to be happy, and do what
    you can to create relationship harmony.

* Stop nursing grudges and start remembering
    why you love your mate and
    work on growing that love.

* Stop burdening your relationship with guilt
    about past events
    and start fresh now by healing that guilt.

* Stop worrying about the future of your relationship
    and start savoring each present moment
    with your mate.

* Share what you love: do something each day
    to create and reinforce happiness
    between you and your partner.

* Share what you think: your mate cannot read
    your mind or know your thoughts unless
    they hear your words.

* Share what you do: allow your mate to share
    in your victories and
    console you in your defeats.

* Offer to take your mate out for dinner unexpectedly
    to give them a both a break and a treat.

* Offer to sit with the children so that your mate can
    spend quality time with their friends or family.

* Offer to give your mate an extra long hug or
    an extra log kiss just because
    you love them so deeply.

EXAMPLE: One mate decided to improve their relationship by practicing compassion and doing many of the things on this list. They did so to see if their marriage could be improved with these free but priceless actions. Of course, it worked and both mates started doing these practices.

2- About Becoming More Compassionate

"True compassion means not only feeling another's pain but also being moved to help relieve it." (Daniel Goleman)

Are you ready to be more compassionate? You can cultivate it if you want to:

* **Uplifting Practice:** What wisdom can you share to make things better, especially with your mate? If you have had the same problem and can share how you solved it with someone else, this is true compassion. If you hear a negative complaint and you can turn it around into a positive solution, this is true compassion. If there is no opportunity for words, can you just smile at someone who looks unhappy?

> If you can do all these uplifting things every day, day after day, this is extending compassion.

* **Similarity Practice:** What do you have in common with whoever you meet, especially with your mate? When you focus on how you are like another - by saying to yourself "just like this person, I..." - this opens your heart to compassion. When you focus on what you have in common, this opens the other person's heart to compassion.

> Remember that we are all human and this automatically gives everyone something in common with everyone else despite any seeming differences.

* **Empathy Practice:** Can you walk for a moment in someone else's shoes, especially your mate's? Can you understand why they are feeling pain? Can you realize this person is lashing out at you because they are hurt and this has nothing to do with you?

> If you can put yourself in the other person's place, especially your mate, this is compassion. The more you can feel empathy for others, the more compassion you can extend to them... and the more love you can give to yourself.

* **Frenemy Practice:** What you can do to think and feel about enemies as friends? When you have an enemy (someone who wronged you in the past), they are a reminder of what you do not like or cannot forgive about yourself.

> So forgive what your enemy has done as if you loved them. Extending compassion to an "enemy" makes "you" your own best friend.

* **Reflective Practice:** How did you show others (especially your mate) compassion today? Think about how you treated the people you interacted with whether at home, at work, on the road, in the store, in the bank, at the restaurant, and so on. Regularly reflecting on compassion helps you to be better at practicing and experiencing it.

> Ask - How well did you do in expressing compassion today?

Ask - What did you learn from showing compassion today?
Ask - What could you do better tomorrow?

EXAMPLE: If you have not seen the "Groundhog Day" movie, then you should check it out. This movies illustrates how compassion can make a person attractive. Only when the main character works on making himself the best he can be, does his attract the love that he has desired for so long.

Tools Part 4: Becoming Your Mate's Best Friend

"One of the most beautiful qualities of true friendship is to understand and to be understood." (Seneca)

If you and your mate want to become best friends, this is what it will take...

* **F - Forever:** A "forever friend" is described by Cicero as one who "improves our happiness and lessens our misery by the doubling of our joy and the dividing of our grief." A "forever friend" is there for you in "fair and foul weather".

* **R - Relaxed:** A friend is someone you can come "home" to. With a true friend, you can relax, put up your feet, let down your hair, and take your ease. If you have to be other than your true self, then you are not relaxed. "Peace at day's end and comfort at life's end" are the ways friends help you relax.

* **I - Identification:** A friend is someone you can identify with and relate to. As the dictionary says, a friend is "a person whom one knows, likes, and trusts; a person with whom one is allied in a struggle or cause; a comrade; and a person who supports, sympathizes, or empathizes" with you.

* **E - Enduring:** "A false friend thinks the friendship over at the first argument while a real friend knows that it is not a friendship until after the first fight." Successful friendships take time to develop and those which endure will have high points and low ones, good and bad days... but they will still endure.

* **N - Natural:** True friends are "natural and easy" with one another. The first test of "true friendship is when silence between two people is comfortable." The second great test of friendship is this: "a real friend is one who walks in when the rest of the world walks out." True friends pass both these tests.

* **D - Dependable:** A friend is someone you can always rely on, always count on, and always trust to have your best interests at heart. A friend "watches your back", has you "covered", is "there for you" no matter what, and is as dependable and reliable as the "sun in the morning and the moon at night."

EXAMPLE: A husband and wife had been drifting apart for a number of years. When the wife fell ill, all of her friends arranged to visit her day and night. Her husband was always "too busy" to visit her at the hospital. When she was discharged, her friends took her home. After this, the wife realized that her husband was not and would never be her friend, so she left him. Too late, he realized what he had lost. So, if you want to keep your spouse, start by doing your best to become your mate's friend.

1- Importance of Liking Your Mate

"Over the course of time, in a relationship, liking is harder to sustain than loving is." (Anonymous)

Do you love your mate but do not like them? Can that even happen? Yes, it can. If you cannot like your mate, you will fall out of love with them.

* **Rational vs Irrational:** Love is based upon feelings and emotions while liking is based on logic and thoughts. This means that love is essentially irrational because the *"heart has its reasons that reason cannot know" (Pascal).*

> Liking is very rational. When asked, one individual can give reasons as to why they like another. Although lovers like to think they have reasons for loving one another, the truth is that they create reasons to explain their love, rather than having fallen in love based on reasoning. So liking almost always has a firmer basis "in reality" than loving does.

* **Commonalities vs Love:** Shared values, outlook, interests, and temperament, are what help one person like another. Love can bind hearts together even when the lovers share none of the things that create liking between people. The more mates have in common, the more they can like each other.

> When you love someone, you can care for them despite the fact that you share little in common. Liking usually has a firmer basis than loving because it is based in reason and not emotion.

* **Objectivity vs Love:** When we like someone, we can be objective about them. Our objectivity with those we like serves to create healthy boundaries between us and our friends (that is compromised by feelings for our lovers).

> With friends, our minds are not clouded by what our bodies have deeply experienced with mates and our brains are not fogged by the chemical haze that comes along with passionate sexual intimacy. With friends, our minds are not restricted by notions of duty. With friends, our feelings do not convince us to "let things slide" as they often do when it comes to lovers.

* **Honesty vs Love:** When we like someone, we can be more honest with them than we can be with those we love. Since those we love mean more to us, we are fearful of saying or doing something that will cause them to walk away.

Yet, the need to manage our love relationships is what usually drives us to seek help from those we like... who we often confide in more! This is the main reason why liking usually has a firmer basis than loving.

EXAMPLE: One mate asked their spouse for a divorce. The mates agreed to wait until their only child went off to college. The other mate decided - in the time that was left in their marriage - to do their best to be a friend to their mate. This individual did so without any expectation of saving their marriage. Yet, that is what happened... and the couple fell in love with each other all over again.

2- Winning Your Mate's Friendship

"The only way to have a friend is to be one." (RWE)

Do you want to win friends? People will line up around the block... when you decide to become a friend. Your mate will be the first in line.

* **Show Genuine Interest:** If you want to have a friend, you need to start by becoming a friend. There is just no substitute for being genuinely interested in others. When you show interest in others, they will automatically start showing interest in you. When you show interest in them, people will line up to become your friend. This is especially important when it comes to your mate.

* **Details Show Genuine Interest:** When you take the time to remember people's names, to know important details about them (like their spouse's and children's names, their hobbies, their interests), and to use all these facts in conversation, this shows your genuine interest in them. They will remember you and consider you a friend. Mates love it when you remember their details.

* **Listen First, Talk Later:** If you want to cultivate a friend, encourage that person to talk about themselves. Make sure that you listen to what they are saying. This is how you gather the details about others that will help you to form a friendship with them. When you listen to others first, others will be happy to be your friend later. Start by asking your mate about what is important to them.

* **Share Common Interests:** If you want to cultivate a friend, discuss what the other person is interested in. They will be happy to share their knowledge and passion with you. You will learn something. If you share common interests with others, you will have lots to share that you both will be genuinely interested in. If you have no common interests with your mate, it is best to cultivate some.

* **Champion, Cheerleader, Coach:** If you want to cultivate a friend, make the other person feel important and do it truthfully. Be their champion by trying to understand their point of view. Be their cheerleader by applauding their successes. Be their

coach by offering advice when they ask you for it. This is very important when it comes to your mate.

* **Positive and Upbeat:** *"Smile and the world smiles with you. Cry and you cry alone." (Anonymous).* A big part of friendship is being friendly, positive, and upbeat. When you smile, when you are positive, when you are upbeat, people will love being around you. They will be proud to be your friend. When your mate is proud to be your friend, your relationship will stand the test of time.

EXAMPLE: The most solid marriages are those where the mates are best friends. Many people believe that mates cannot be friends, but that is not true. You should be able to expect as much from your mate as you do from a close friend. You should be able to like and trust your mate as much as you do a friend. You should be able to count on your mate as you do on your best friend.

Tools Part 5: Building Solid Relationships

"A successful marriage requires falling in love many times, always with the same person." (McLaughlin)

If you and your mate want to build a solid relationship, here are some tips:

* **Rules:** Relationships cannot function properly without simple, clearly stated rules about what you need your marital partner to do and not do.

> An example of "what to do": if you value honesty highly, then tell your mate they MUST be honest with you at all times. **No lies!**
>
> An example of "what not to do": if you are a private person, then tell your mate you do NOT want them to share with others anything that could be considered as "confidential".

* **Routines:** Relationships work best when they are supported by routines designed to keep the love flowing between the mates.

> For example, whenever mates part from one another, they should hug and kiss upon leaving. When together, they should sit close to one another and hold hands. Each day they should make a point of saying something kind to each other. On special days, there should be gifts or enjoyable activities.

* **Responsibilities:** Relationships work best when there are clearly defined responsibilities that are fairly divided between the mates.

> For example, if both work, then both need to do their share of household chores. An unequal division of labor will drain the passion out of even the most committed relationship. Marriages work best when each mate is doing their fair share of the work (and they end when this does not happen).

* **Relatives:** Relationships work best when mates can agree on how to handle their relatives. Marriages work best when mates act as a united front and put each other first before other relatives, even children and especially in-laws.

> For example, disagreements about parenting will break apart even the most loving of relationships. Disharmony with in-laws and other relatives will have the same effect.

* **Romance:** Relationships cannot function properly without romance. Love and romance are the ultimate marriage builders.

> For example, mates who do not enjoy regular romantic getaways with one another will drift apart if they do not often reconnect as lovers.

EXAMPLE: If there is one thing you can do to rebuild your romantic relationship that is to have regular getaways. Even if you cannot leave your home, have your children visit your relatives.

It is all too easy for mates to be so focused on being parents that they forget to be lovers. Mates who forget to be lovers are at high risk for getting a divorce. If you do not want to get away with your mate for a romantic outing, then your romantic relationship is over with for all intents and purposes.

Tools Part 6: Key Messages of Love and Romance

You will know that your communication is good when you and your mate can honestly believe the following about your relationship:

1- *"You Are My Number One"* - which is what your mate wants to be.
- Instead of being "too busy" for love and romance.

Most relationship books focus on the differences between men and women (and focus on how to "bait and hook" each gender). Yet both men and women - although they come at relationships differently - want the same thing out of them. Each wants a happy connection with the other.

While men might use intimacy to get sex and while women might use sex to get intimacy, they both want to know that same thing. They want to be FIRST in each other's lives. They want to be "number one" with each other.

Here are some quick ways to show your mate they are "Number One":

- Wear your wedding ring or something
 your mate gave you.
- Keep your mate's picture on your phone
 and at your work.

- Compliment your mate - routinely –
    in front of others.
- Refer often to your mate in conversation
    with others.
- Mouth "I love you" to your partner across
    a room full of people.

- Thank your mate whenever they do
    something for you.
- Ask your mate's opinion and advice
    on even small matters.
- Listen to your mate even
    when it is inconvenient.
- Hug your mate to the count of 30
    (no need to count out loud).
- Always kiss before leaving home
    and after arriving home.

- Be a united front when
    you both are out in public.
- Be a united front with relatives when
    you both are in private.
- Defend your mate when others
    (even family) criticize them.
- Support your mate in the achievement
    of their dreams.
- Give your mate undivided attention
    when they ask for it.

In all you do, make sure your mate knows they are your "Number One".

2- _"You Are Always on My Mind"_ - which is what your mate should be.
- Instead of just simply "forgetting" to be romantic.

Most romantic relationships die because mates take one another for granted. Mates forget what a gift they are in each other's life.

Men tend to become focused on their job-career-work and, by chasing money-status-fortune, they lose sight of their relationship. Women tend to become focused on their children-homes and, by getting caught up in the daily crush of parenting-household tasks, they lose sight of their relationship.

Once mates become primarily focused on what lies outside of their relationship, they stop putting attention on nurturing their relationship. Their romance dies because the relationship is no longer on the mates' top priority.

Here are some quick ways to show your mate they are "on your mind":

- Contact your mate at times when they do not
    expect you to.
- Leave a love note in their purse-wallet
    where they will find it.
- Send an email just to say "I love you:
    I am thinking of you..."
- Send a text just to say "I was thinking of you...
    that's all."

- Always let your mate know if and
    how long you will be late.

- Leave a sexy message on their
    personal voice mail.
- If it is a day special to your mate,
    be sure to celebrate it.
- Before an important day at their work,
    wish your partner luck.
- Email your mate a link about something
    that interests them.
- Laugh at your mate's jokes
     (even if you have already heard them).

- Cheer when your mate does something for you
     (clap, shout, etc).
- Call up your mate and volunteer to take on one
    of their tasks.
- Grant a wish that your mate does not expect
    from you.
- Praise your mate on their Facebook or other
    social media page.
- Leave emoticons on their Skype chat with
    a loving message.

In all you do, make sure your mate knows they are "on your mind".

3- _"You Are The One for Me"_ - which is what reassures your mate.
- Instead of letting others "get in the way".

The best relationship advice you can ever get is... to be yourself. The happiest, longest relationships are those when each partner is convinced the other is "the one" for them. That they are mates... meaning that there is a soul connection between them.

Many relationship advice books try to get you to be someone else to manipulate your mate into the relationship. Yet this cannot work because mates in long lasting marriages are attracted to one another based on who they are inside.

The only happy relationships that last are those where each mate wants to be with the other because of who they are inside. They want to know and believe that their partner is the one for them.

<u>Here are some quick ways to show your mate they are "the one" for you:</u>

- Wedding rings with your names
    engraved on them.
- Have photographs of you both displayed
    all over the house.
- Get monogrammed towels,
    napkins, and sheets.
- Have doormats and house signs
    with your names.
- Put a "stick figure" decal on your car
    representing your family.

- Record a greeting on your voice mail
    with both your voices.
- Participate in an activity that you
    both like to do.
- See a movie that each of you
    likes and discuss it.
- Go to events where each of you performs
    (like sports or plays).
- Take a romantic getaway with
    your mate at least twice a year.

- Put all important events on a shared calendar
    you both follow.
- Watch videos of important events
    shared together.
- Revisit spots where you dated,
    became engaged, got married, etc.
- Celebrate important anniversaries
    (not just your wedding!).
- Tell your mate what you like - specifically –
    about them.

In all you do, make sure your mate knows they are "the one for you".

4- <u>*"You and I Are a Team"*</u> - which is what comforts your mate.
- Instead of "arguing" try romancing.

The promise of marriage - that mates will stand by one another "for better or for worse", "for richer or for poorer", "in sickness and in health" - is what mates want out of their relationship.

Each mate wants to know that the other one will be there for them... no matter what. Great relationships depend upon communication, kindness, and trust to sustain them. Showing loyalty is a form of kindness which builds trust and enables meaningful communication between committed mates.

<u>Here are some quick ways to show your mate that you "are a team":</u>

- Always act as if your mate was present and watching you.
- Always put your mate first before others (even your children).
- If someone else criticizes your mate, come to their defense.
- If your children try to divide you and your mate, do not allow it.
- If your in-laws try to divide you and your mate, do not allow it.

- Never see a potential romantic interest in private.
- Never accept an expensive gift from a romantic interest.
- If you get a romantic communication, show it to your mate.
- If someone puts moves on you, say no and tell your mate.

- Make it clear to those all around you
   that "you are taken".

- Keep your wedding ring in
   clear view all the time.
- If your mate picked out your clothes,
   be sure to tell others.
- If your mate gave you your clothes,
   be sure to tell others.
- If you had a great vacation with your mate,
   brag about it.
- Share breakfast and dinner with your mate
   as often as possible.

In all you do, make sure your mate knows that you "are a team".

5- *"You Still Touch-Move-Excite Me"* - which is the essence of romance.
- Instead of saying you are too tired for lovemaking.

Remember that great lovemaking always comes from a deep bond with a loving mate. Lovemaking is supposed to get better - more exciting, more connected, more warm, more intimate, and more passionate - as time goes on.

Great lovemaking is the result of a great romantic relationship! Unless each mate has warm romantic feelings for one another, those sparks cannot burst into the flames of mind blowing passion.

The truth is there will always be others who are younger, better looking, richer, etc than you... but there will only be a few individuals than anyone can truly connect with... and feel moved and excited about.

Here are some quick ways to show your mate they "move-excite" you:

- Watch a movie together
    that gets you in the mood for love.
- Tell your mate how good looking they are
     (be specific as to why).
- Encourage your mate to wear clothes
    which flatter them.
- Each decides which is their mate's favorite body
    part and why.
- Each makes a video about why
    the other is sexy.

- Play the "Twister" game with your mate
    to get physically closer.
- Play the "Strip Poker" game with your mate
    to enjoy undressing.
- Play the "Chocolate" game: each true answer
    earns a chocolate.
- Each mate acts out their personal sexual fantasy
    with the other.
- One gives clues to the other as to where
    sex toys can be found.

- Take every chance to kiss your mate...
    this is an opening for loving.
- Take every chance to give a hug to your mate...
    this is an opening for love.
- Take every chance to cuddle with your mate...
    this is an opening for loving.
- Take every chance to caress your mate...
    this is an opening for loving.
- Take every chance... for love!
    Seize romantic moments when they come.

In all you do, make sure your mate knows they "move-excite" you.

Tools Part 7: 100 Romantic Text Messages

If you want to get good communication flowing between you right away, then pick up your phone and send your mate a text message.

Here are some you can choose from... to use in almost every situation.

Messages from the Heart

You have the key to my heart: treasure it
You live inside my heart every day
You and me, my love: here, now and forever
To live in hearts we leave behind is not to die
If ever two were joined at the heart, it is we

Messages of Appreciation

Thanks for loving me even at my worst moments
You are like a rare gem I am blessed to hold
No one else has ever made me feel
    as cherished you have
I feel so warm and alive whenever you are near me
When you smile at me, it is like the sun comes out

Messages Delivering Gifts

You are a precious present I receive every day
My unconditional love is my greatest gift to you
You have been the greatest gift in my life
May I always appreciate the gift of you in my life
Faith, hope, and love are the gifts you give to me

Messages of Gifts of Words

I cherish every kind word you have ever said to me
I am grateful for every kind word you have said
    about me and to me
I keep your lovely words deep inside my heart
I love to hear my name when it comes from your lips
Every one of your compliments is written on my soul

Messages of Inspiration

You bring out the best in me
I live to become ever more worthy of your love
Your love inspires me to be a better person
I am daily inspired by your love and kindness
You are a role model of kindness and compassion

Messages from the Soul

Be mine because I will love you forever
Our love is eternal and immortal
Ours is a forever love: you are my immortal beloved
We can only be separated, never parted
Time will go by but our love will never die

Messages of Trust

I feel love being myself when I am around you
You are the one I trust most in this world
I trust you with myself: all that I am
      and all that I have
I trust you above anyone else that I know
My faith and trust in you are everlasting

Messages about Falling in Love

It is hard to see...
      because I only have eyes for you
It is hard to hear...
      because I keep remembering your words
It is hard to think...
      unless it is about how much I love you
It is hard to touch...
      unless it is your sweet self I am holding
My heart and all that I am is focused on you...
      and you alone
I only have eyes for you
      for you and no other

Messages about Forgiveness

I am sorry... whatever I did/did not do,
    I now regret it
Please forgive me...
    I just was not thinking clearly
I love you...
    for listening to me with an open mind and heart
Thank you... for being in my life and
    for sharing your love
I have learned...
    I promise to do better by you the next time

Messages about Time

1 second without you
    can seem like an eternity
1 minute with you will
    always gladden my heart
1 hour to resolve our issues
    each week is time well spent
1 year to deepen our love even more
    is my birthday wish
1 lifetime together with you is
    all that I really want

Messages for Busy People

Take 3 seconds, close your eyes,
    and feel my love for you
"On my break time, I say a little
    prayer for you"

If I can see a smile from you...
    then I do not need gifts
If I can hear the sound of your voice...
    then I do not need music
If I can touch your hand...
    then I do not need a romantic getaway

Messages to Stop Loneliness

When you feel lonely, dial...
    [the first three digits of your cell phone]
I you still miss me, dial...
    [the next two digits of your cell phone]
If you want to see me smile, dial...
    [the next two digits of your cell phone]
If you need some support, dial...
    [the complete number of your cell phone]
Guess what? I will answer and you will not be alone!

Messages from Hello

H means "How are you? I really want to know!"
E means "Everything all right? I really want to help!"
L means "Love you more than you know!"
L means "Love you: You are my best friend forever!"
O means "Obviously I miss you when we are apart!"

Messages from Good Bye

G means "Go but come back as soon as possible!"
D means "Do love the one who loves you the most!"
B means "Be checking in with me once a day!"

Y means "Yes, I miss you terribly... come home!"
E means "Everything is so lonely without you!"

Messages of Support

Whenever you feel blue, I will be there for you
Whenever I feel blue, all I have to do is think of you
Whenever you feel sad, I will try to make you glad
Whenever I feel sad, for you, I will always be glad
I will be there for you whenever you call me

Messages on the Edge #1

"If you think I'm sexy,
    come along and tell me so"
You know what I want...
    come into my bed and give it to me
You know what I need...
    and please come home as soon as possible
I need you in me right now
    ("nights are forever without you")
Our favorite place + our favorite position =
    heaven on earth

Messages on the Edge #2

I wish I was your blanket, snuggled in your bed
I wish I was the pillow just underneath your head
I want to be around you, I want to hold you tight
I want to be the one who kisses you good night
I want to be the one who wakes up beside you

Messages about Everlasting Friendship

I will love you until the end
I will always be your true friend
I will gladly share your ups and downs
I am always going to be around
Until the end, I will be your best friend

Messages about Ingredients of Love

I made a special brew especially for you
Into the special brew, I added in 1 huge hug
Into the special brew, I mixed in 2 big kisses
Into the special brew, I sprinkled 3 cups of love
I hope my special brew, stirs your heart, I do!

Messages about What Love Is

Love is special, sweet, and makes life complete
Love is giving, kind, and gives me peace of mind
Love is joy, caring and increase when sharing
Love is mostly laughter and seldom tears
Love is more than words express: it is happiness

Messages for Holidays

You make every day Valentine's Day for me
Valentine's Day celebrates the love uniting us
You make every day like a New Year's Celebration
Our anniversary is the day when life began for me
You make me feel like it's Christmas when I see you

Messages for Birthdays

We were born to be together...
    we are so lucky
Our anniversary is really
    my second birthday
As your birthdays come and go,
    you mean more and more to me
On your special day, know how special
    you have become to me
On the day you were born,
    the angels made my dream come true

Messages from Authors

"You must allow me to tell you how
    ardently I love you." (Jane Austen)
"Love is composed of a single soul
    inhabiting two bodies." (Aristotle)
"...only one happiness in this life,
    to love and be loved." (George Sand)
"Love is shown in your deeds,
    not in your words." (Jerome Cummings)
"Being deeply loved by someone
    gives you strength, while loving someone
    deeply gives you courage." (Lao Tzu)

Messages from Lovers

"Mine eyes desire you above all things."
    (Catherine of Aragon)

"Soul meets soul on lover's lips."
    (Percy Bysshe Shelley)
"The best thing to hold onto in life is one another."
    (Audrey Hepburn)
"With all thy faults, I love thee still."
    (William Cowper)
"To love and be loved is to feel the sun
    from both sides." (David Viscott)

Messages from Poets

"you are my sun, my moon, and all my stars."
    (e. e. cummings)
"Make me immortal with a kiss."
    (Christopher Marlowe)
"My night has become a sunny dawn
    because of you." (Inb Abbad)
"The sight of lovers feedeth those in love."
    (William Shakespeare)
"The love I've often spoken my dying lips shall
    speak." (Eugene Field)

MYSTERY BONUS

Visit Us at:
http://www.soulmatelovesecrets.com/bonus.htm

When you arrive at this link, the bonus of "120 Romantic Ideas" will be waiting for you. These romantic ideas will help you and your mate to grow closer! Romance will help your communication!

120 ROMANTIC IDEAS

www.soulmatelovesecrets.com

For more information visit us online at:
http://www.soulmatelovesecrets.com
Check out our Facebook Page:
https://www.facebook.com/soulmatelovesecrets

About the Author

"Those who cannot remember the past are condemned to repeat it." (George Santayana)

Over the 6,000 years of recorded history, people have learned - through trial and error - what has and has not worked to create and sustain successful romantic relationships. Many of the best relationship creating techniques have been lost over the course of this history.

Since 1990, Ellen Arlene Mogensen has researched what history teaches about what has and has not worked when it comes to creating and sustaining, happy, long term romantic relationships. Ellen has rediscovered many romantic techniques which have been timed tested and proven to work.

Since 1996, Ellen Arlene has helped her clients to heal a wide variety of relationship problems such as communication issues, parenting conflicts, lifestyle differences (conflicts over work, money, cleanliness, religion), sexual dysfunction, and recovery from relationship damaging events (infidelity, rape, loss of children, disability in children) using her historical research as a guide.

Ellen Arlene has helped her clients attract and find their special soulmate. She has helped marriage partners to resolve their differences and save their family. She has helped loving couples to rekindle the spark between them. She has helped parents to more resourcefully raise their children.

All by using ancient relationship wisdom to help solve modern problems.

Contact Information

Soulmate Love Secrets

Ellen Arlene Mogensen
532 Old Marlton Pike,
c/o Fun Life, PMB 248
Marlton, NJ 08053 USA

Web: http://www.soulmatelovesecrets.com
Email: ellen@soulmatelovesecrets.com

CPSIA information can be obtained
at www.ICGtesting.com
Printed in the USA
BVHW091145041118
532123BV00018B/652/P

9 781720 402527